The Greatest Leap of Your Life:

Simple yet Difficult

Richard E. Pugh

Copyright © 2010 by Richard E Pugh

The Greatest Leap of Your Life
Simple Yet Difficult
by Richard E Pugh

Printed in the United States of America

ISBN 9781612153414

All rights reserved solely by the author. The author guarantees all contents are original and do not infringe upon the legal rights of any other person or work. No part of this book may be reproduced in any form without the permission of the author. The views expressed in this book are not necessarily those of the publisher.

Unless otherwise indicated, Bible quotations are taken from The King James Version of the Bible; The *Holy Bible*, New Living Translation (NLT). Copyright © 1996 by Tyndale House Publishers, Inc. Used by permission; The Revised Standard Version of the Bible (RSV). Copyright © 1952 [2nd edition, 1971] by the Division of Christian Education of the National Council of the Churches of Christ in the United States of America. Used by permission; and *The Living Bible* (TLB). Copyright © 1971 by Tyndale House Publishers, Inc. Used by permission.

www.xulonpress.com

The Greatest Leap of Your Life: Simple yet Difficult

	Page
Dedication	vii
Preface	ix
Introduction	xi
I. Some of Life's Leaps	17
II. The Difficulty of the Greatest Leap: Infinite vs. Finite	30
III. The Importance of the Leap to You and God	47
IV. Why Did Christ Come to Earth?	65
V. The Holy Spirit: The Bridge for Your Leap	86
VI. Born Again: The Process That Sustains Your Leap	106
VII. Joy and Peace That Is Real	123
VIII. Our Responsibility—Keep the Leap Flowing	142
IX. The Second Coming of Christ	194
Epilogue	211
Sources	217

Dedication

I am so grateful for the opportunity to write this book. First and foremost, I thank God for His guidance in the process of writing the many drafts leading up to the culmination of a finished product. I wish to thank Brenda Pitts for her invaluable initial critique of my first final draft and Sharilyn Grayson for the excellent copyedit before my submission for publication. Judy Beard was wonderful and patient in typing a number of the drafts over a nearly two-year period, and very timely in doing so.

I also wish to thank my pastor, Dr. Craig T. McClellan, who reviewed my first draft and offered a number of very helpful notes and suggestions.

In memoriam, I wish to thank my best friend from my early childhood days, Joseph Hosay, after whom we named our son. Joe's impact on me is a vital part of this book.

And last but certainly not least, I wish to thank my wonderful family. I am so in love with them! I am so blessed in what each of them has given me in life. They were all so helpful in reading my first draft and offering very constructive thoughts. They include my wife, Judy; my children: Kim, Christy, and Joey; my niece, Mal; and my son-in-law, Matt. All have contributed in one way or another to the final shape and format of this book.

I pray that this book will in some way lead many to a better understanding of God's plan of salvation for all of us and personally accept it for themselves.

Preface

The objective of this book is to break down the important components of Christianity into very understandable sequences that bring to light God's plan of salvation for all of us through the life, death, and resurrection of His Son, Jesus Christ. This book is not a theological treatise on Christianity. I'm not trained as a theologian or capable of navigating such deep waters.

Instead, this book is a reflection of the basics of Christianity written in a simple manner by a very common Christian. I hope that the story of how Christ has influenced my life and brought me insight, peace, and a simplified understanding of God's plan of salvation provides insight to others.

Acceptance of His plan is critical for our salvation, and it requires a leap of faith that is simple, yet difficult for many. I hope to help mitigate a good deal of that difficulty, particularly in the first few chapters that focus on leaps of faith in our lives and the distinction between the infinity of God and the finiteness of mankind.

I also hope that this book attracts those on the fringe, those who are looking for greater meaning for their lives, and those who superficially understand the concepts of Christianity or may call themselves Christians yet haven't found the strength and peace in life that Jesus promised.

All of us seek an end to our restlessness and the peace and joy to help us not only to cope, but to thrive in a world that often seems difficult or overwhelming.

This basic Christianity 101 book attempts to enlighten others in finding a meaningful relationship with God and Christ that they can grasp firmly and nurture for the rest of their lives.

Introduction

I have never been one to wear my religion on my sleeve. Some Christians, perhaps many, might be critical of me for this tendency. And rightfully so. I consider myself susceptible to criticism in that I have kept from others the opportunity to hear my testimony or thoughts on the importance of God, Jesus Christ, and the Holy Spirit to my life and the great strength, peace, and security that God has brought me and that I know He can bring to others. Simply put, I've been unintentionally selfish.

I have improved at this fault over time, and if engaged in a discussion about religion or God, I have not hesitated to talk about my faith. The main reason I began writing this book is that I wanted my family to understand the foundation of my beliefs more completely. Certainly, my immediate family knows of my faith, but we never dwell on it. I've never wanted to turn anyone off from God and Christ by being overbearing in pushing my beliefs on others. Although I don't believe I ever have, I certainly haven't been an effective advocate, either.

As I continued work on the first draft, I decided to write something like a personal experience account or narrative that actually might be more interesting to read for those beyond my immediate family. This work is certainly not a memoir, as I have not lived a life that would even remotely draw that sort of interest. But I have recorded my experience with issues and problems that are similar to what we all face in life.

As you will soon learn, this book is not an academic treatise written by an intellectual giant. It is a simple book written by an ordinary guy, a layman's book written by a layman. Though I've used a number of biblical quotes and references to helpful books, I have in no way written a systematic theology. Not only am I not even close to being qualified to expound on theology, but even if I were, that direction would divert attention from the concept I had in mind while preparing this book. And that concept is this: despite the complexities of this world, including the intricate depth of

The Greatest Leap of Your Life

theology, life is meant to break down complex things into simple components for day-to-day living. As complex as man can seem to be (just think of the complexities of our bodies and minds), most of us are the same. We have some desires in common: we all yearn for truth, love, simplicity, and a sense of peace. Abraham Lincoln once remarked that, "God has to love the common man; he made a lot of them." I'm certainly one of them.

I have no doubt that the Holy Spirit has guided me in this sharing of my faith, helping me to offer what I sincerely believe in a straightforward manner. This simple book deals with a simple but powerful faith in a complex world. I believe that I have an important message that I want to reach others. I hope that considering the truth about God, Christ, and the Holy Spirit as I see it more than fifty years after I was born again touches some readers. Hopefully, the different slants or vantage points in any repetition help bring clarity and reinforcement to my convictions that may help others find their Lord and Savior.

I will tell you that I have been greatly influenced by a man that I believe God has blessed as a gift to the world: Billy Graham. When he burst onto the scene in the late 1940s, many Christians and non-Christians alike viewed him with a jaundiced eye. Yet he has withstood the major test of time, not only for the strength of his convictions and consistency of both his message and his life, but for his meticulous determination to oversee his ministry from the beginning with professional auditors and managers to maintain the integrity of his organization's work for the past sixty plus years. Thus, his preaching and his conduct have given him a reverence in this country and the world that is unprecedented. The "Counselor to the Presidents" recently celebrated his ninety-first birthday.

Jesus declared that His message must reach all nations before His return. Because of organizations like Billy Graham's, this goal has been largely accomplished. I hope I'm not committing sacrilege to say that I personally have considered whether Billy Graham is God's second John the Baptist blessing to the world before Christ returns.

I hope that what I have written will help at least one person who might not otherwise have done so to find and accept Jesus Christ as Lord and Savior. Though I feel deeply blessed in this life and have been very fortunate in so many ways, my family and I have faced difficult circumstances, like all families in this world, only a few of which I've noted. I intend to strike a balance of content and conciseness that brings simplicity to the complex and keeps the reader's attention to leave him clear direction to lasting joy and peace in his life through Jesus Christ.

We all have faced difficulties in life, and we will continue to experience them. At times these challenges may seem mundane, while at other times they can appear to be overwhelming. For some, life may seem boring or oppressive, creating a lack of enthusiasm and even depression. God does not want us to be overwhelmed, bored, depressed, negative, or lost in this world. His infinite love for us is beyond our comprehension. He awaits our call to Him. As I describe how I found God and Christ, why the evidence leads me to believe that God wants us to be happy and at peace here on earth and for eternity, how He has impacted my life numerous times, and how you can find peace and joy in your life, I hope and trust that you will find the link to God and Christ that enables you to take the greatest and most rewarding leap of your life.

Chapter I

Some of Life's Leaps

Following a protracted period of time putting together an outline for the book's content, as I put pen to paper for the first words of this chapter, I went to my den and located the 1984 edition of the *Funk and Wagnalls Dictionary* (sorry, but that's when our kids needed it) to look up the word "leap."

As a verb, among other definitions are the following: "1) To rise or project oneself by a sudden thrust from the ground; jump; spring. 2) To move, react, etc., suddenly or impulsively. 3) To make an abrupt transition: to leap to a conclusion."

The Greatest Leap of Your Life

As a noun, among other definitions are: "2) The space traversed by leaping. 3) A place from which a leap may be made. 4) An abrupt transition."

The predominance of these definitions implies that we often make leaps in life without a lot of forethought or consideration. Perhaps that conclusion is unfair on my part. Personally, I've seen people devote considerable thought before taking one of a number of leaps we all take during the course of our lives. The connotation for "leap" in my mind for this chapter and this book is that important leaps pertain to a transition of great importance that is not necessarily easy to do, one that may perhaps seem impossible for some. But if accomplished, the new direction and awesome rewards can change life completely.

Some Leaps in Our Own Lives

Just think about some of the leaps that might have occurred in your life or others. As you do so, note that some appear to have greater safety nets than others.

How about that marriage proposal? Guys, when you asked your bride to marry you, did you have doubts along the way that delayed the actual proposal? Did she? Did you

The Greatest Leap of Your Life

ever have a doubt or two for a while after your proposal? Did she? Nevertheless, when you both took that leap toward marriage, you believed and she believed that the decision was right for both of you.

When you think about it, a proposal is a huge step in life! At the point of a proposal, what do we really know about marriage? Certainly, in many cases, we observe our parents from a limited perspective and know a little bit about how they make it work. But what do we really know at that point about the effort necessary to maintain a happy marriage for both husband and wife? Not very much actually. Only when we wear those shoes ourselves do we begin to grasp its challenge and gratification. Certainly, genuine love goes a long way in facilitating the challenge of developing and maintaining a good marriage. That kind of love enables generosity and sacrifice for one another on a regular basis.

What about children? Do we want them, and can we agree on how many? Do we have any idea of the work involved? Or can we begin to imagine the incredible joy and love we have before us when they come into the world?

Do we really understand the economic challenges that raising a family brings and the various stages of that economic commitment that peaks when the kids are off to college? Just a couple of years ago, one of my alma maters became the first in the nation to cost over $50,000 annually!

So much more complexity followed the leap of faith we took with that marriage proposal, and more is still to come. Marriage in some ways parallels life with its ups and downs. However, with the right choice and strong commitment, the pluses far outweigh the minuses in the leap that we take with so many unknowns.

What about that employment selection or change? We all want to get ahead in life, as we should. We would like to improve our lot in life, and we want to provide well for ourselves and our families. Our work ethic, education, experience, and capabilities all play very important roles in how well we advance in life, not only in compensation, but also in finding work that brings enjoyment and satisfaction in what we are doing and accomplishing.

Along the way, we may be enticed to make changes for a promotion within an organization or with a new company. While accepting a promotion in the same organization, we may face uncertainty as to whether we can handle the greater responsibilities. The promotion may lead to a whole new set of circumstances, including reporting to a new boss. What will that new relationship bring? Should we have stayed where we were feeling comfortable and secure?

We may even change course and go into something entirely new, such as starting or joining a new business. In evaluating a new start-up business, we need to know our initial and continuing costs and how much we need to borrow to get the business off the ground. Is there a market out there to sustain success? We no longer will have a guaranteed weekly income, even though success may in the long run garner much more than if we hadn't taken this leap.

Whatever the circumstances in life, we consider taking chances with leaps that have uncertainties because we can't possibly know everything about decisions we make during our time here on earth. Just like the proposal and eventual marriage, we are not all-knowing, and we are all imperfect. But we are still willing to take the leap because our mind and heart agree that there is hope in the future it offers.

Choosing a college for teenagers and their parents is no small task either! The competition is severe in this realm, and this process consumes prospective students and their parents during a student's junior and senior years in high school. Academic and geographic considerations, as well as sports or artistic interests each have a major role to play in the selection. And as much as we don't want to admit it, the matter of the prestige of different schools adds to the peer pressure. When all is said and done, hopefully these young people have a number of good choices. Just think of the pressure of making a decision about where to spend the next several years of their lives! Yet, they only have access to a finite or limited amount of information on whether the selection they make will turn out to be a good one and the best one for their future. Nevertheless, they must make the decision, regardless of the uncertainties.

And purchasing a home requires a buyer to analyze a variety of factors. Some of these are empirical enough so that the buyer can factor the cost into the family budget and make a decision or take a leap that appears quite logical. Yet he can't enjoy the total certainty that signing the papers is or was a safe thing to do. The interest rates could go up if the loan is variable. He might lose his employment unexpectedly. Some unanticipated major expense might explode on the scene, or a breadwinner could incur a lengthy sickness. House values could plummet, as they did in 2007 and 2008, when the economy tanked due to subprime mortgages and the abuse of our capitalistic economic system by a few that hurt so many. Yet we try our best to understand what appears

The Greatest Leap of Your Life

to be the right decision. We don't necessarily want to hold ourselves back just because we encounter unknowns.

Serious illness may hit a family. When it does, you have to consider your options. Are you with the right doctor and hospital? If you are uncertain, how do you go about getting a second opinion? What are the best resources for treating this illness, and can you get an appointment to be seen if that makes sense? After this research and further evaluation, you now have to make some decisions on what is best for you. These decisions are not always crystal clear, but at least you have put yourself in a position to make the best possible decision you are capable of making. Yet a leap of faith lies in whatever direction you take.

Making a decision about joining the military has been an important decision for many. When I was in the midst of completing my graduate degree in Washington, D.C. (1966–1968), I realized that the military was realistically the next step because of the Vietnam War. The political atmosphere then was very turbulent, with the March on the Pentagon, antiwar demonstrations throughout the country, hawks and doves in the Congress, and political candidates running on the major issue of Vietnam. Martin Luther King, Jr. was assassinated in April of 1968. I remember every day, for

The Greatest Leap of Your Life

a week or two, seeing the smoke rising out of the nation's capital from my Alexandria, VA., apartment during the days following his death, a result of emotional riots and burning in Washington and many other U.S. cities. Bobby Kennedy was likewise assassinated that June, immediately following his primary victory in California in his run for the presidency.

For me, there was no doubt I was going into the service; it was just a matter of when and at what level. I wanted to serve, and therefore I finished my MBA degree work a bit early and graduated mid-year in February 1968. I received my commission in the Army in early April and finished my basic training in San Antonio, Texas that June. I had decided to seek a commission as an officer and serve for three years while using my education to my advantage, as well as that of the Army. The other choice would be to wait to be drafted as an enlisted man and serve for two years. Almost certainly, either choice would involve service for one of those years in Vietnam, as approximately half a million troops were there at the time.

My decision was certainly not heroic; instead, it was pragmatic and likely safer. I happened to believe in the war, and so I did want to serve there in a capacity where I could be effective, wherever in Vietnam that might be. As it turned out, the three years I served in the Army did take advantage of my education, as I worked one year at William Beaumont Army Hospital in El Paso as Administrator to the Chief of Surgery, one year at the 67th Evacuation Hospital in Quin Nohn, Vietnam, and the final year at the Surgeon General's Office in Washington, D.C.

The most important year by far was the year I served as part of the team at the 67th Evacuation Hospital. As you can imagine, the team and its dynamics changed because we soldiers were all overseas for twelve-month tours. But although we were always coming and going, the mission, objectives, and high level of professionalism remained steady. We were a cohesive group providing the very best of care to severely wounded soldiers. We were the main support for An Khe, where the Army was conducting heavy duty missions every day for many years.

Serving with this group and doing my small part to serve these very brave men was one of the great privileges of my life, as well as an incredible learning and sharing experience. I saw first-hand the atrocities of war. My first day at the hospital, as I was reviewing the roster of patients, one case in particular struck me: a young man named Mark who lost both of his legs to a land mine. Later that day, I went up to

The Greatest Leap of Your Life

the intensive care unit to visit with patients and staff. I will never forget looking at this handsome, blond soldier lying in bed with the stumps of both legs surrounded by two wire baskets. It was such a sad image and reality to think that this war could have so negatively impacted Mark's life. Another image that never faded occurred when I was walking from BOQ (Bachelor Officers' Quarters) to the hospital. The back door to the triage center burst open as a soldier on a gurney was being rushed to an adjacent building, the Operating Room (OR). I ran to open the doors to the OR for the group, and as I looked down, I saw a young soldier with nearly half the left side of his face blown off. His injury was gut-wrenching to see. I couldn't stop thinking about what this victim must have felt. I will never know.

What I do know is that working at this hospital was a privilege beyond words. Our team of devoted professionals worked hard and, yes, played hard. We developed some of the greatest relationships of our lives in that setting. We were a family that supported one another and, most importantly, supported our troops, doing some wonderful things to save their lives. That outcome, however, was not always possible. I remember one of our thoracic surgeons from South Carolina coming back to the BOQ one evening with his head down, looking depressed. Several of us gathered in his room to make sure he was all right. He wasn't. He began to talk, and before long his shoulders were heaving in a devastating cry because he had just lost a soldier on the operating table. These tears he shed and great sorrow he felt didn't trouble him because he had done something wrong. No, he knew that he had done all he could. He sobbed because he so badly wanted this soldier to live and heal and go home, but his injuries were too severe to be mended in the OR.

There is so much to learn and gain out of life, despite the many uncertainties, as we take a variety of leaps that contribute to the direction of our lives. I am so grateful for the leap or decision I made in joining the Army at the time I did.

The Smaller Leaps

While these leaps in life are very big and important ones, we all make other so-called leaps here and there throughout our lifetime. Perhaps these decisions don't require quite as much consideration, because the impact one way or another isn't likely to be as drastic. For example, we've all heard people say "I took the leap and dyed my hair. I hope I'm going to like it." Or, "I took the leap, traded in that favorite convertible of mine, and invested in a more economical and dependable car." Or how about this one: "I took the leap and called that girl I met Friday night to see if we could go out. Man, was I scared making that call." Now here's one of my leaps that most people would agree fits the less important category, while some rabid baseball fans would label it in the mega-category, and some others would call me a traitor. In 1971, I changed my rooting affiliation from the Yankees to the Red Sox! My Yankee fan friends still scratch their heads on that one. Suffice it to say, the range of leaps we take in life is broad, and the impact of the results or consequences varied.

The Greatest Leap

However, I am convinced that one decision is the greatest and most important leap in the world. And that decision is to accept the truth that God sent His only Son, Jesus Christ, who was both divine and human, into this world to teach us how to live through His word and example, while performing miracles of compassion and power, to die on the cross as a substitute and atonement for our sins, and to rise from the dead so that those who believe in Him as their Lord and Savior might have life more abundantly (spiritually) here on earth and life eternal in heaven.

I acknowledge that this leap is not a slam-dunk for most people; in fact, it is quite difficult for many. Why is taking this leap of faith in accepting this truth both so important and so difficult? I'll attempt to address this question in the next chapter.

Chapter II

The Difficulty of the Greatest Leap:
Infinite vs. Finite

Life and Mind

First, let's begin by talking a little about life itself and the different levels of happiness and satisfaction that exist among the human race. For many, life is something of a constant roller coaster. To illustrate, think about the following: we might get excited one day because we're going shopping for something very special, heading to the golf course on a beautiful day, leaving for an exotic vacation, expecting our kids home for the weekend, planning how to spend the IRS check that just arrived, exulting over a wonderful review we just received from the boss, or marveling at one of the greatest blessings in life: a newborn child. Most lives include much excitement, but they also experience disappointment, disillusionment, and unhappiness as well.

On the down side of life's roller coaster are very difficult things that can affect lives, including death, disease, accidents, poverty, addiction, child and spousal abuse, divorce, loss of employment, loneliness, depression, fear, and much more. Just reading the newspaper daily or turning to the TV news sometimes bewilders us with so many bizarre killings, accidents, and unfortunate circumstances that people encounter each day. All of the above can devastate the individuals and families affected.

Throughout any society, some people exude and feel great confidence in themselves; they are very independent and ready to handle any and all challenges for a good part of their lives. Others who have a similar confidence also realize their imperfections and their inability to control and properly adjust to all circumstances in life. Still others have little confidence in themselves and find life a much more difficult challenge. These descriptions are but a few of the many different levels of mental outlook on life.

Regardless of where you fall in that very broad spectrum, the fact of the matter is that all of us are restless when we sense things aren't quite right in our world. Sometimes we're affected by the lack of material things; perhaps many times that's the case. But it's been proven that material things are limited in bringing ultimate happiness in people's lives. I'm convinced that the greatest restlessness is in our spiritual lives, our souls, which affect significantly our mental outlook on life.

If we are honest with ourselves and we have something of a conscience, we will acknowledge that we are continually sorting out a myriad of signals and feelings that run through our heads throughout the day. In this process, we try to determine how we feel about different people, different situations, and different environments, and how we can best react to them. Ultimately, how we deal with these sources of fact and emotion throughout our daily lives significantly impacts the satisfaction and peace we find in life.

As part of our imperfection, we are people with egos that have a distorted sense of our control over the circumstances and realities of life. Our pride in our intelligence and accomplishments often leads us to believe we are invincible, no matter what the challenge or event before us. When not carried too far, all of the above valuable traits are important to who we are and what we can accomplish in this world.

A Stumbling Block to the Greatest Leap: Pride

Of the above, I think that pride in our intelligence and accomplishments is perhaps the biggest stumbling block for mankind to take the leap that God sent His divine/human Son down to earth to die for us and our sins and to rise from the dead, so that we who believe can have life eternal with God and greater joy and peace here on earth.

Let's focus on this hurdle of man's intelligence and accomplishments. Look what man has developed and accomplished over the years. A review in my 1984 Funk and Wagnalls Encyclopedia renders something of an interesting abstract from a long list of notable inventions and breakthrough discoveries beginning in 1590:

Compound microscope	1590	Automobile engine (two-cycle)	1879
Telescope	1608	Mimeograph	1887
Steam turbine	1629	Kodak camera	1888
Barometer	1643	Gasoline automobile	1893
Steam engine	1705	Diesel engine	1893
Piano	1710	Motion picture projector	1894
Spinning jenny	1764	Airplane	1903
Automobile	1770	Gyroscope compass and stabilizer	1910
Power loom	1785	X ray tube	1916
Cotton gin	1793	Insulin	1922
Small pox vaccination	1796	Penicillin	1928

The Greatest Leap of Your Life

Steam locomotive	1804	Twin rotor helicopter	1936
Stethoscope	1819	Turbo-jet engine	1941
Electric motor	1821	Atomic bomb	1945
Reaper	1831	Electronic digital computer	1946
Telegraph	1837	Transistor	1948
Photography	1839	Hydrogen bomb	1952
Ether	1846	Solar battery	1954
Water turbine	1849	Sodium cooler nuclear reactor	1957
Elevator	1852	Communications satellite	1958
Gyroscope	1852	Laser	1960
Machine gun	1861	Artificial heart (left ventricle)	1966
Typewriter	1868	Human heart transplant	1967
Telephone	1876	First complete synthesis of gene	1970
Internal combustion machine	1877	Skylab orbiting space laboratory	1973
Microphone	1877	CAT scanning	1975

Volumes and volumes have been written about the enormous advances that have been made by man, particularly over the past fifty years, and we could safely bet that these inventions will continue to escalate. We could compile so many different lists of accomplishments. In addition to the above, we can go back to the late 1600s to Sir Isaac Newton's theory of gravity; Einstein's twentieth-century work with the powerful atom; the cadre of people who created the atomic bomb in the 40s and the use of atomic energy since; the astronauts standing on the moon in 1969, paving the way for space stations later; the continuing advancements of speed and memory in the computer world; and the incredible advances in medicine to save lives and make the quality of life much better as people age. More recently, in 2008, the Associated Press reported a fascinating experiment:

> The world's largest particle collider successfully completed its first major test by firing a beam of protons around a 17-mile underground ring Wednesday in what scientists hope is the next great step to understanding the makeup of the universe ...
>
> After a series of trial runs, two white dots flashed on a computer screen at 10:36 a.m. indicating that the protons had traveled the full length of the $3.8 billion Large Hadron Collider. ...
>
> An organization, known by its French acronym CERN, began firing the protons—a type of subatomic particle—around the tunnel in stages less than an hour earlier.
>
> Now that the beam has been successfully tested in clockwise direction, CERN plans to send it counterclockwise. Eventually two beams will be fired in opposite directions with the aim of recreating conditions a split second after the big bang, which scientists theorize was the massive explosion that created the universe.
>
> The project organized by the 20 European member nations of CERN has attracted researchers from 80 nations. Some 1,200 are from the United States, an observer country which contributed US$531 million. Japan, another observer, also is a major contributor.
>
> The collider is designed to push the proton beam close to the speed of light, whizzing 11,000 times a second around the tunnel.

Smaller colliders have been used for decades to study the makeup of the atom. Less than 100 years ago scientists thought protons and neutrons were the smallest components of an atom's nucleus, but in stages since then experiments have shown they were made of still smaller quarks and gluons and that there were other forces and particles.

The CERN experiments could reveal more about "dark matter," antimatter and possibly hidden dimensions of space and time. It could also find evidence of the hypothetical particle—the Higgs boson—believed to give mass to all other particles, and thus to matter that makes up the universe.

I provide the detail from this article to emphasize that mankind is gaining ground in his understanding of a very sophisticated complex body of knowledge, which cuts to the very core of the universe. Just recently I read in an Associated Press article by Seth Borenstein about findings presented at the Astronomical Society convention indicating that the Milky Way is as large as the Andromeda galaxy, thus reversing decades of scientific thinking. This incident demonstrates the continual advancement of man's intelligence as he learns more and even disproves some theories developed in an earlier period.

Continuing in the present, America realized more than ever in 2008 how important it is to cease our dependence on foreign oil. We will hopefully put our best minds on developing alternative forms of energy, such as solar, atomic, wind, and natural gas (of which the United States has an abundance) to handle our energy and transportation needs more effectively. These needs represent more and more opportunities for us to use our intelligence and find satisfaction in new achievements that hopefully make for a better world.

There is no doubt about the intelligence and ingenuity of the human race. So, considering this record of accomplishment that has required hard work and weathered many failures before success, mankind unsurprisingly has a pretty sizable pride in its intelligence and capabilities. As a result, leaps of faith are not necessarily big on our agenda.

Finite versus Infinite

Think about it, why would an intelligent, accomplished human being believe the unlikely chain of events that God set in motion? If he even believes in God, why would he believe that God could possibly create a plan to send His Son Jesus Christ to earth, in the combined form of God and man, and do so via immaculate conception involving a woman named Mary? Then the plan continues that His Son lives a very modest and quiet life, including making His living as a carpenter, for thirty years before He begins His three-year ministry, which ends with His death by crucifixion at age thirty-three. This "silly story" contains other elements that are difficult to swallow for many with great pride in their intelligence.

Jesus makes wine out of water (His first observed miracle); makes the blind see; heals the lepers and enables the crippled to walk again; feeds a crowd of five thousand at the Sermon on the Mount, beginning with two fish and five loaves of bread and ending with several baskets of leftovers; and brings people such as Lazarus back from the dead. He heals through touch, as in the story of the hemorrhaging woman, or remotely, as in the case of the Roman captain's daughter. He walks on water and calms the angry sea with a command. He knows more Scripture than the educated and learned Pharisees and scribes, yet He never went to school. And to top it all off, God lets Him die the most shameful of deaths, crucifixion, and then He rises from the dead three days later. Come on; how naive do we expect sophisticated mankind to be?

Well, I propose that a key hurdle for most people to accept the truth about God and His Son Jesus Christ is the difficult choice to accept God as infinite and mankind, His children, as finite. Man is so engrossed in the material things he has and the challenges he has conquered and will continue to conquer that he often neglects to take the time required to think about the existence of God, whose infinity of power and love dwarfs the capacity of a finite mankind. An infinite God can and does love beyond our comprehension and does have the power to do and create anything He chooses, far beyond humankind's capacity. As long as man continues to reject that God exists or attempts to limit Him through the criteria of the human microscope, then he will always crash against this major stumbling block that will prevent him from taking the greatest leap of his life. How does mankind get past this obstacle?

That same Funk and Wagnall dictionary defines infinity as, among other things: "1) Having no boundaries or limits; extending without end. ... 3) All embracing; perfect; infinite wisdom."

It defines finite as, among other things: "1) Having bounds, ends, or limits. 2) That may be determined, counted, or measured. 3) Subject to human or natural limitations: our finite minds."

I believe that God is infinite and we are finite. The distinction between the two is enormous and probably indescribable and unimaginable because we are incapable of defining or conceiving of the enormity of infinity with our finite minds. Let's start by looking at the enormous differences in power and capacity of some finite things we can comprehend.

> A gigantic ocean wave vs. a lake ripple
> A gentle breeze vs. a hurricane
> A golf cart vs. a jet airplane
> An exploding firecracker vs. a hydrogen bomb

The difference in power and capacity between infinite vs. finite is not fully comprehensible to the human mind, but it certainly dwarfs the distinct differences of the above.

When and if you consider that this distinction is true, then that truth can break down the barrier against believing that God indeed is capable of the divine conception that led to the birth of Jesus Christ as the divine/human being He was. Further, you can then accept that Jesus did have the capability to perform all of the miracles that were witnessed and documented in the Scriptures. Only when we look at Jesus in the finite microscope of His being a human being without a divine nature as well do we have trouble believing the revelations about Christ in the Bible and become skeptics.

Humankind's Intelligence and God's Science

I have a simple theory about our intelligence and God's infinite capacity that created the earth with all of its complexities. I believe that God has always existed and has always known that He would create man in His image. As part of that image, He wanted man to have free will to make important choices in life, including whether he chooses to believe in and worship God and His Son. But He also wanted man, among other pleasures, to enjoy himself on earth through his work. Therefore, He created earth with great complexities to explore that would keep man challenged, resourceful, and actively learning how to use his intelligence to unravel the mysteries in nature and science that enabled us to make all of the significant advances we have made in the world's infrastructure, management systems, communications, medicine, technology, defense systems, space exploration, agriculture, and the like. Now we can add to that list the ecology of cleaning up the environment that imperfect man has polluted and, in the USA, trying to eliminate dependence on foreign oil.

I believe that God envisioned this progress because the process is healthy for the enhanced satisfaction and happiness of His children and because these accomplishments can bring good to the world. Despite the incredible mysteries that He has allowed us to solve, I believe that we will never exhaust the complexities and mysteries still remaining on this earth to be solved because an infinite God intended it that way.

As we make these discoveries, mankind requires a multitude of skill sets to put these breakthroughs to practical and useful purposes each day; we need to work as a team, developing and maintaining relationships with others. God wants us to have fellowship among ourselves, but very importantly, He wants us to have fellowship with Him. I think we can thank an infinite and loving God for: the blessings of work opportunities; the free will with which to make choices in life; and the ability to use our capabilities in concert with our fellow human beings to make this world a better environment in which to live. God not only desires that we have fellowship with Him, but He also recognizes how important fellowship is with our family, friends, neighbors and co-workers.

But happiness and satisfaction in life depends on more than work, family, recreation, and material things. God created man in His own image. God is a Spirit, and the most important part of a human being is his individual spirit. The human spirit craves peace and joy, and if it doesn't find it, it lives in uncertainty and restlessness. We will look at this spiritual hunger later and explore why accepting Jesus Christ as Lord and Savior is the key to finding peace and joy that is real, exhilarating, consistent, and the foundation for great contentment here on earth and throughout eternity.

Taking the Leap

The average self-sufficient individual finds difficulty in leaping from a life of independence to an acknowledgment that he has a Creator who can help him in life's walk and promises to do so.

But the fact of life is that, as strong, wise, and independent as we consider ourselves to be, we are not as in control of our lives as we think. Yes, we should plan, using our blessings of intelligence, education, and experience to help us in life and our life's work. But we should also understand that life is far more difficult and complicated than we know. Total reliance on our individual capacities to deal with all of the challenges and needs we will face in our lifetime will fall short. And it will come up shorter in the most difficult of times. I am not saying that we should just sit back and sulk and wait for God to do everything. I do not accept escapism. God expects us to use our capabilities and blessings throughout our lives. Jesus expressed this thought repeatedly in many of the thirty-six parables recorded in the Gospels. I am simply acknowledging that, even with our capabilities, we are imperfect, dependent, spiritual, and limited, and that a powerful, loving God is always available for those who seek His help.

We have souls that need to satisfy the restlessness inherent in each one of us, which is the essence of who we are. We desperately need goodness and happiness that power, prestige, and material things can never fully provide. We yearn deep inside to find a consistent, dependable peace and joy.

Some of us realize this reality early in life, while others do later in life, but some of us unfortunately never realize it at all.

We are very important contributors to our ultimate destiny in life here on earth and life eternal, but we are not its complete creators. We cannot control all events, circumstances, accidents, diseases, or exciting and happy occasions that occur in our life. Anyone who thinks he can is sadly mistaken.

The kind of leap that we need in order to get off the total independence track that many of us run is one of faith and trust in something far bigger and more powerful than ourselves. Taking that leap will help us not only to weather a crisis, but also to enjoy daily and appreciate even more the existing blessings we have in life. Our restless soul craves this relationship naturally because God, who is a Spirit, created us in His image. We have a spirit that craves happiness and peace. He wants us to find happiness and peace, and He wants us to love and follow Him.

I believe that we find room for independence with limits as we embrace the dependence on God that can thrive in our lives. To paraphrase a well-known quote, "Let us try to address those opportunities and challenges before us and change or support what we can, and leave to God those we cannot." I personally believe that this proper approach to life can give God's children a great support system as we all attempt to use our blessings and capabilities as best we can throughout our lifetime.

Thus, we can simply sum up the great leap as follows. An infinite God created finite man in His own image, including giving him a spirit. He blessed His children with the intelligence and free will they needed to live their lives in a complex and challenging world. That free will can be a two-edged sword, as man has the ability to accept or reject things in life, including faith, love, and sin.

The great leap focus in this book is whether we humans can accept the existence of an infinite God with a plan for salvation for us, which I will attempt to define simply with illustrations beginning in the fourth chapter. In the third chapter, I want to discuss why the great leap you may take is so important both to you and to God.

Chapter III

The Importance of the Leap to You and God

Life Can Be Difficult

Life is complex and difficult in many ways, and it seems to become more so with the explosion of information, technology, distractions, and issues that proliferate in our lives. Getting caught up in that complexity and conflict in life can be confusing, stressful, and damaging to each one of us. At the time of this writing, people are still deeply affected by the mess of the subprime loan explosion that triggered Wall Street losses, affecting the pensions and savings of millions of Americans and other people around the world. In turn, these losses have triggered layoffs, a depleted housing market, and mortgage foreclosures that dramatically impact the families affected. And just in the last few months, the explosion of an oil rig that has leaked massive amounts of oil into the Gulf of Mexico and onto some of its shores has deeply impacted the lives and economy of the Gulf Coast in Louisiana, Florida, and Alabama.

God's Road Map

Despite God's infinite knowledge, wisdom, and power, I believe that His road map to happiness and peace in this world is meant to contain simple basics which, if accepted and adopted, have a way of producing security, confidence, peace, and joy within a world of many uncertainties and challenges. This road map is not an escape route from life, but rather a "compass" for our lives provided by our Creator because of His love for us.

God does not want His children to live unhappy, stressful lives. He has created a plan that can lay the foundation to live in peace in this world and tackle its challenges with a strength that enables us to withstand whatever comes our way.

God has promised to those who accept His plan of salvation that He will never give us more than we can handle, as long as we maintain our faith and trust in Him. The Bible in Matthew 11:28–30 KJV says that Jesus proclaimed, "Come unto me, all ye that labour and are heavy laden, and I will give you rest. Take my yoke upon you, and learn of me; for I am meek and lowly in heart: and ye shall find rest unto your souls. For my yoke is easy, and my burden is light."

God also had a plan for the entry and ministry of Jesus: the birth in Bethlehem and His life as a child and carpenter in Galilee. God had a plan for preparing the way for Christ through the man in the wilderness, who gained a following with his preaching about repenting from sin immediately in order to prepare for the coming of the Messiah. God meant for John the Baptist to prepare the people for something very special to come.

When John the Baptist's disciples came to John to complain that Jesus was now baptizing the people and taking away John's following, he made the following powerful statement recorded in John 3:27–36 NLT:

> God in heaven appoints each person's work. You yourselves know how plainly I told you that I am not the Messiah. I am here to prepare the way for him—that is all. The bride will go where the bridegroom is. A bridegroom's friend rejoices with him. I am the bridegroom's friend, and I am filled with joy at his

success. He must become greater and greater, and I must become less and less.

He has come from above and is greater than anyone else. I am of the earth, and my understanding is limited to the things of earth, but he has come from heaven. He tells what he has seen and heard, but how few believe what he tells them! Those who believe him discover that God is true. For he is sent by God. He speaks God's words, for God's Spirit is upon him without measure or limit. The Father loves his Son, and he has given him authority over everything. And all who believe in God's Son have eternal life. Those who don't obey the Son will never experience eternal life, but the wrath of God remains upon them.

God understands the nature of the free will and intelligence He has granted us. He knows the rewards and risks for mankind. He especially understands that both can lead to a lack of commitment and faith on our part in response to His plan for our salvation. Why? The combination of intelligence and free will can lead to a great sense of independence within our lives. We may think we can dictate the terms of a meaningful relationship with our Creator, if we in fact believe in God at all. This assumption can conflict with our accepting His plan for our salvation and with establishing the discipline required to maintain the communication with

Him necessary to drive a deeper relationship and a growing faith in something greater than ourselves.

God's Premium on Faith

As part of God's great plan and wisdom, He places paramount importance on faith, prayer, and acceptance of His Word in the Bible. Perhaps He does so because these acts all revolve around trust in Him, which can be difficult for finite man, as our infinite God understands. Think about the difficulty. We have never seen God. We have never seen Jesus Christ, though we have substantial evidence that He lived and performed the myriad miracles that He did, including rising from the dead. His body was never found, yet He appeared to many people, including His disciples several times, following His resurrection, over a fifty-day period leading up to Pentecost.

We have all heard the term "doubting Thomas." When Jesus first appeared to His apostles following His resurrection, they were astonished and joyful. The apostle Thomas was not there at that time. When Thomas returned, the apostles excitedly told him of the Lord's visit, yet Thomas would not believe them. He said something to the effect that until he could see the scars of the crucifixion on Christ's hands and place his hand in the hole in His side, he would not believe. John 20:26–29 NLT records the following scene:

> Eight days later the disciples were together again, and this time Thomas was with them. The doors were locked; but suddenly, as before, Jesus was standing among them. He said, "Peace be with you." Then he said to Thomas, "Put your finger here and see my hands. Put your hand into the wound in my side. Don't be faithless any longer. Believe!"
> "My Lord and my God!" Thomas exclaimed.
> Then Jesus told him, "You believe because you have seen me. Blessed are those who haven't seen me and believe anyway."

I consider this incident to be such a powerful message from Jesus concerning the premium God places on faith and trust in Him. Jesus knew that virtually all future believers would not have seen Him in their lifetimes. We are now two thousand years beyond His life and resurrection. He laid the foundation for hope, reassurance, and expectation for all of us who followed His death and have never seen Him in these words—"Blessed are those who haven't seen me and believe anyway."

In our finite world, we regularly encounter things that we don't see but believe. We accept electricity as being real, but we don't see it. We believe in love, but we can't see or touch it. We acknowledge the speed of sound, but we can't touch or see it. We know of air but we can't touch, see, or hear it. The speed of light has been measured, but we can't see or touch it. Thus, a number of finite things in this world that we can't see or touch are very important parts of our lives, and we believe that they exist.

Thus, if we can believe or accept these finite entities, some of which can't be seen, heard, or touched, why can't we accept other realities created by an infinite power?

Well, the fact is that many can't believe. They have great difficulty taking the leap of believing that an all-powerful God with an infinite love and strength exists. I believe that God places so much value on faith and trust for the very reason that it is not easy for His intelligent and accomplished children, whom He has given free will through His creation of each one of us, to reconcile the magnitude of God and His plan for salvation to the everyday tangibles of life. We have such an easier time accepting as real those things we can touch and feel and hear with our finite minds. However, when we do accept God and His plan for our salvation, the reward is great and powerful.

The Lessons of Faith and Trust from Children

Think about how proud we are of our children when they do good and difficult things. We don't think about this fact very much, but just consider the incredible trust our little children put in us to put food on the table, maintain a place for them to sleep, help them learn right from wrong, kiss a booboo to make it feel better, and lift their spirits when they have had a bad day. They expect us to love them. I believe that God intended us to learn from our children what He wants and expects from us. He expects the same love, trust, and faith in Him and Jesus Christ as we expect and have received from our young children. Somehow, it seems so much easier for our children to have such faith in and love for their parents than it is for us adults to reciprocate with this same love and trust for our Father in heaven.

When Christ's disciples tried to keep small children from interfering with Christ's time, Christ rebuked His disciples by saying to them that they needed to have a strong yet child-like faith in the Kingdom of God. Christ's teachings had such depth that even today theologians and others are unraveling some of their complexities, yet their most important fundamentals are so simple that even children can grasp them. The paradox of such a faith is therefore extraordinarily meaningful to our Father in heaven, becoming the first step in a wonderful journey through life here on earth and life eternal, when we accept His plan of salvation and grow in our faith through the power and fellowship of prayer with God.

Ephesians 2:8–9 KJV declares the grace of faith: "For by grace are ye saved through faith; and that not of yourselves: it is the gift of God: not of works, lest any man should boast."

My interpretation here is that, while our good works here on earth are very important to accomplish for the betterment of this world and our fellow man; good works alone will not gain us eternity. Only faith in God and His plan for salvation is necessary. The grace is from God; the faith is up to us. Interestingly, when we have taken that leap of faith, we learn to become better people, and our good works only multiply.

Can Your Faith Be Too Late?

I think it important to understand that it's never too late to make that leap, while realizing that you may lose the opportunity to do so if you continue to put it off. I'd like to put forward two stories here in support of this position. One is an important, insightful parable from Jesus concerning the vineyard workers, and the other is a personal experience relating to my dad.

Consider the following parable from Jesus concerning the vineyard workers, a story that reflects God's willingness to accept all into His kingdom, no matter how late in life they accept His plan for salvation.

> For the Kingdom of Heaven is like the owner of an estate who went out early one morning to hire workers for his vineyard. He agreed to pay the normal daily wage and sent them out to work.
> At nine o'clock in the morning he was passing through the marketplace and saw some people standing around doing nothing. So he hired them, telling them he would pay them whatever was right at the end of the day. At noon and again around three o'clock he did the same thing. At five o'clock that evening he was in town again and saw some more people standing around. He asked them, "Why haven't you been working today?"
> They replied, "Because no one hired us."
> The owner of the estate told them, "Then go out and join the others in my vineyard."
> That evening he told the foreman to call the workers in and pay them, beginning with the last workers first. When those hired at five o'clock were paid, each received a full day's wage. When those hired earlier came to get their pay, they assumed they would receive more. But they, too, were paid a day's wage. When they received their pay, they protested,

"Those people worked only one hour, and yet you've paid them just as much as you paid us who worked all day in the scorching heat."

He answered one of them, "Friend, I haven't been unfair! Didn't you agree to work all day for the usual wage? Take it and go. I wanted to pay this last worker the same as you. Is it against the law for me to do what I want with my money? Should you be angry because I am kind?"

And so it is, that many who are first now will be last then; and those who are last now will be first then.

Matthew 20:1–16 NLT

I believe that there is more than one message here. The message most important to me is that God loves us so much that even the person who doesn't take the leap until later in life will receive the same life eternal with God and Christ as the person who may have accepted and lived this truth for a longer period of his earthly life. Jesus is saying that we have no right to begrudge that gift if our heavenly Father wishes to love so well all who accept God's plan of salvation.

My Dad

However, God's patience and generosity do not change the fact that putting off this acceptance does put us at risk that

The Greatest Leap of Your Life

the moment to do so again may never come again. Secondly, those who take this leap of faith earlier in life benefit from true peace, joy, and security for a longer period here on earth as well as a more rewarding spiritual life that they can share and enjoy in their relationships with family and friends.

Reflecting further on this truth, I would like to share a story about my Dad. He was a very good father who was something of a paradox in his personality. He was a very emotional man who could tear up easily when watching a touching story on TV or in a movie or encountering significant real life matters. I will always remember calling home after I landed at an Air Force Base in the state of Washington upon my return from Vietnam. While my parents knew I was returning after the completion of my tour, such a phone call would be, of course, special to them. My Dad picked up the phone, and I said, "Hi, Dad, I'm home." I heard only dead silence for what seemed like thirty to forty seconds before he was able to say something in response. He was overwhelmed by the moment. Perhaps this sensitivity related in some way to his gift of expressing emotion with his beautiful baritone voice. While he had no formal training or promoter to manage him, he rose to an upper level of musical accomplishment. He was good enough in 1949 to get on the Ted

Mack Amateur Hour, broadcast nationally, but he did not win. Probably his greatest compliment and potential opportunity relates to the CEO of IBM, the first Tom Watson.

In the upstate New York community known as the Triple-Cities (Binghamton, Johnson City, and Endicott), my dad had earned an outstanding reputation as a singer with a very good baritone voice. IBM had initiated a presence in Endicott by the 1940s, and one weekend IBM invited Dad to sing the national anthem before a big celebration at their Endicott country club facilities. Tom Watson was there. Following my dad's singing of the national anthem and before he could leave, Mr. Watson dispatched one of his aides to invite my dad to his private box to join him for the evening's festivities. At the end of the evening, Mr. Watson said to him, "Vernon, here is my card. I will be in town for two or three days; call me at this number. I want you to come to work for IBM and become an important part of our traveling IBM chorus." I'm sure Mr. Watson had become a man of the arts and recognized outstanding quality in a singing voice.

Well, my dad never called Watson. I think that Dad remained loyal to his current employer, Endicott-Johnson Shoe Company, for a number of sentimental reasons. And of course, IBM was not quite yet the incredible corporation that it was to become.

I spoke of the paradox of my father's personality. The other side of him corresponded to that emotionalism in that he was a very impatient man with a significant temper. He was never physically abusive, but he could be overbearingly verbally abusive. This inconsistency of his personality made life for my mom difficult. At times, he would display a warm, affectionate personality which could change on a dime into anger and impatience. My mom, in contrast, was a remarkably patient, loving, and gentle lady.

In the late 80s, my dad was diagnosed with prostate cancer. He began to take a turn for the worse in the summer of 1991. I, of course, kept close contact with him, my mom, and my sister. My parents had moved to Clearwater, Florida, in the early 80s, as did my sister and brother-in-law. I will always remember talking with them on a dreary late fall Sunday afternoon as I was closing down our modest cottage in Massachusetts. Following that conversation, I remember sitting down on the step of our deck, looking down the lake, and sensing that his condition did not sound right and that his time left may be very short.

The Greatest Leap of Your Life

Having already made an airplane reservation, I went to work Monday morning to clear my calendar for the week with my assistant, Sherry Buzcek. Then I asked Jim Phillips, a co-worker in the financial department at my work, to drive me to La Guardia Airport.

I had for many years prayed to God that He would touch my father's heart for Christ. However, things never seemed to change. On the flight to Florida, I penciled an outline of what I wanted to say to my dad, who knew he was dying. I wanted him so badly to be in Christ before he died. This desire is my greatest prayer for my whole family. I actually kept those notes, and here is the outline which notes exactly what I said to him and my mom in his bedroom shortly after I arrived.

> Benefitted by love of parents who supported me throughout my life
> Benefitted by the education they provided me to give me an occupation that I love and by which I have been able to support my family nicely
> I have a lovely wife and children, two daughters and a son
> I have two lovely homes
> I am a very lucky man to have all of this, and I have much for which to be grateful
> All of these things can be taken for granted and do not guarantee happiness

The Greatest Leap of Your Life

But I know that God has reminded me of how lucky I am, and I do believe He's made me appreciate these blessings far more than I would otherwise
What is most important to me is my faith and trust in Jesus Christ

— What makes it so important?
God came down to earth as a human being, and while He was here He taught us a way of life He wished us to live. God's presence here on earth was in the flesh of Jesus Christ
The most important part of this truth is that God's and Jesus' mission was to show us through Jesus that He loved us so much that He was willing to go through a torturous death for us so that death could be defeated and we could have life everlasting and life more abundantly here on earth
First, we have to understand what God is. He is a Spirit, and He has set high standards of what He expects from His children. He also wants our love and devotion. But He doesn't want it from robots; He wants it from His creations, whom He has given free will to choose as they may
We can't meet the standards He set for us by ourselves. But we can do so much better with His guidance and strength, which comes through genuine trust and belief that we can have life everlasting as well as life more abundantly here on earth, simply by trusting that God's Son died for us - He rose from the dead for us to defeat death, and He gave us His continuing presence through the Holy Spirit
I think, among all of the many joys and tribulations of our children, God gave us an opportunity to understand better what He expects from us. Just as we, as little children, trusted our parents in what they told us

and that they would provide for us, that's what God expects from us as human beings
It's that leap of faith that is so difficult for us to make and to continue to live
But if we don't lose that faith - with God's help - it can easily be done.

Well, as it turned out, my talk with him was not necessary. When I finished, he told me that a pastor had been visiting him for a few months and that he had accepted Jesus Christ as his Lord and Savior. I was so grateful to know of his decision. His life change was remarkable. Later that evening, I heard him say to my mother, "Louise, I am so sorry for how I have treated you. As much as I love you, I know I have been very difficult to live with; I hope you can forgive me."

My dad died on that Thursday, and I am convinced that, because of God's incomprehensible love and forgiveness, he is in heaven with his Lord and Savior. For that assurance, I am forever grateful. I do wonder how unhappy my dad must have been in dealing with his anger and impatience and how much good he could have done, along with his outgoing personality, had he let Christ come into his heart much earlier to tame that emotionalism and channel it into positive directions. But I remain so grateful that in his last days he did find the truth and blessings of his Savior.

God Cares for All of Us

God seeks for all of us to have a peace and joy in our hearts, and He recognizes how difficult it is for some to find their way to the cross through faith and trust and how difficult it is for some to pray. Because He acknowledges this hurdle, it is important and joyful for Him and incredibly rewarding for us when we take that leap of faith and learn to have solid fellowship and growth with God through prayer. This leap is founded on the fact of God's love and the fact of Jesus Christ: His life, His death, and His resurrection.

Whether you have taken the great leap or still remain uncertain, gaining more depth in your understanding of God's plan of salvation for us is important. In the next chapter, we will focus in more depth on why God's Son had to come to earth.

Chapter IV
Why Did Christ Come to Earth?

I have heard an enlightening little anecdote that may seem a bit silly, yet for me and perhaps others, it may provide a simple parallel illustration as to why God sent His only Son into this world. A man who was walking along a sidewalk happened to look down at the sidewalk as he finished taking a certain step and noticed that he had just stepped on an ant hive. He stopped and looked down at the now crushed and scattered hive. As he looked more closely, he found himself filled with empathy for some of the ants who were struggling to keep from being crushed. They were in trouble and in need of help. He conveyed later to a friend that he wished he could become an ant in order to communicate with them to help them understand their plight better and lead them to a safer place. Obviously, this man was very sensitive. This anecdote for me is an analogy to God's own sensitivity and love for mankind as He observed our own predicament here on earth as lost souls in so many ways. He chose to become like one of us through the birth and life of Jesus Christ to help us find our way to Him for guidance and salvation. A biblical excerpt that relates to this idea comes from Hebrews 2:14–15, 17 NLT:

> Because God's children are human beings—made of flesh and blood—Jesus also became flesh and blood by being born in human form. For only as a human being could he die, and only by dying could be break the power of the Devil, who had the power of death. Only in this way could he deliver those who have lived all their lives as slaves to the fear of dying.
> Therefore, it was necessary for Jesus to be in every respect like us, his brothers and sisters, so that he could be our merciful and faithful High Priest before God. He then could offer a sacrifice that would take away the sins of the people.

Jesus came down to earth to be like us in order to teach us how to live a better life with peace and joy and learn to become more like Him. In order to comprehend more fully why Christ came to earth, we first must understand more about God.

Created in God's Image

God is infinite, and He is perfect. He is a Spirit with an infinite love that is not fully comprehensible to our finite minds. Therefore, we will never fully appreciate the true depth of God's love for us, but we can learn that it is at least as deep as we can possibly imagine.

But He is also holy, and He hates sin more than anything in this world. And because He created us in His image, we have a spirit that lives within each one of us. This spirit, or soul, becomes our conscience over the course of our lives. As it develops, it becomes the essence of who we are. Our spirit is challenged, refined, and developed throughout our lives within our individual environments. Our spirit affects how we think and act and impacts our mindset and the values that guide our everyday lives. And with this spirit, we must address how we deal with sin and the other challenges of life.

The other important part of being created in God's image is that He gave each one of us a free will. God is a Spirit of great love, and He wants very much for His children to love Him, not as robots with no emotion, but with real love offered in free will and filled with emotion.

We must realize that being created in God's image does not make us infinite, like God is. We are finite and therefore not all-powerful and perfect, as God is. We are thus imperfect and dependent upon Him. I know that some do not believe in God, and perhaps many others who believe in God do not believe that they are dependent upon God. But the fact remains that we are imperfect; we all suffer the effects of sin and succumb to sin in our daily lives.

Sin is the greatest threat to a peaceful, exciting, and enjoyable life for mankind. The world has always been filled with temptations for sin, and in this twenty-first century, these temptations seem to have increased enormously from even the mid-twentieth century. So how do we battle an enemy that seems to grow in strength as our society becomes increasingly exposed to distractions and perhaps less attached to a Supreme Being? Where and how can we find help and guidance?

God's Plan

Over the next few pages, let's first understand God's plan of help for us through the life and death of Christ here on earth. God, with His infinite love, looked down upon His struggling children and determined to come down as a man, though divine, in the form of His only Son, Jesus Christ. The Old Testament scriptures proclaimed the coming of the Messiah and described Him numerous times, and John the Baptist in the New Testament predicted the coming of the Messiah, all of which clearly pertain to Jesus Christ. God's objective was for Christ to lay the foundation upon which we could live in a difficult world filled with sin, have life more abundantly here on earth, and find life eternal through faith in Christ's life, death, and resurrection. Christ died on the cross as a substitute for all of mankind's sins. His willing death was the only perfect sacrifice God could accept to reconcile His hatred of sin, our sinful nature, His love for us, and His forgiveness for our sins.

Jesus came down to earth to reach God's children (all human beings) by words and example concerning the high standard that God expects from His children. These standards stressed a number of characteristics or traits of importance. One of those traits valued by God and Christ is humility, as expressed in T. W. Hunt's *The Mind of Christ:*

> The incarnation itself is an act of humility (Heb. 2:16). God had to stoop low to become a man. Everything about His earthly life was lowly. He was born in a stable, and His cradle was a feeding trough.

The circumstances of His life were modest and unassuming. He grew up in a village despised by the people of His day (John 1:46). Had we been writing the script for His story, we would have placed Him in the Jewish capital, Jerusalem, under the best-known teachers of the day. Paul, unlike Christ, was highly credentialed. Yet he said, "For you know the grace of our Lord Jesus Christ, that though He was rich, yet for your sake He became poor" (2 Cor. 8:9). He submitted to His parents and lived in obscurity for thirty years. Try to fathom the enormous significance of this fact: God incarnate anonymously walked the streets of an obscure little town for most of His earthly life. He worked as a carpenter and served the needs of the common rural districts around Nazareth.

Incredibly, He who was perfectly holy submitted to a baptism intended for sinners. One of His purposes was to identify with the lowest and vilest of us. John the Baptist, with keen perception, "tried to prevent Him, saying, 'I have need to be baptized by You, and You come to me?'"

Jesus Christ submitted to His own creation. By virtue of His nature and office, He was inherently higher than the high priest, higher than the governor, higher than Caesar. He was above all humans and human agencies. Yet He gave Himself to the service of others. He expressly said, "For even the Son of Man did not come to be served, but to serve, and to give His life a ransom for many" (Mark 10:45).

His ministry of three years was relatively short, but His teachings were powerful and clear, which was as God intended. His Sermon on the Mount (referred to in Matthew and Luke) is an incredibly concise summary of the standards by which we should strive to live. One section, the Beatitudes, speaks to what Christ and God expect from us in living our lives. Among others, the four Gospels, Matthew, Luke, Mark, and John, contain many other teachings from Jesus' ministry and descriptions of His miracles.

Jesus as God-man lived a perfect life, reflecting His teachings. Yet as a man, He experienced the same emotions and senses that we all have. He felt hunger and thirst, as well as emotions of sympathy for the lepers, blind, and crippled who sought His help. He shed tears over Lazarus's death before He raised him to life again. He felt the pain of the intense thrashings from the Roman soldiers prior to the piercing pain from the nails driven into His hands and feet in His crucifixion. The intensity of this sacrifice has come home to me in a very vivid way through two accounts which I would recommend to those who wish to sense the incredible pain Jesus must have felt as He went through this sacrificial ordeal because of His amazing love for us. One is chapter nine, "Crucified," from T. W. Hunt's *The Mind of Christ*. It is a gut-wrenching read. The other is the Mel Gibson film entitled *The Passion of the Christ*. Jesus took the punishment for our sins so that we could be justified in God's eyes, gaining forgiveness of our sins and life eternal with Him through simple faith in this fact.

I believe that there was a final deeply agonizing part of the crucifixion for Christ and God. For the longest time, I had trouble understanding why Jesus, just prior to His death on the cross, called out: "My God, my God, why have you forsaken me?" (Mark 15:34 NLT). This painful cry bothered me because I couldn't fathom why God would desert His Son, following His sinless life and enormous sacrifice.

As I did more reading and thinking about the crucifixion, it became clear, at least to me, why the connection between Father and Son ruptured. God is holy, and He hates sin more than anything else. He loves His children beyond our comprehension and doesn't want to lose any one of us to eternal damnation. God needed to find the perfect example to teach us to live better, less sinful lives. The only sacrifice possible to justify us, despite the enormity of our sin, for eternity with Him was for His Son Jesus Christ to become that sacrificial lamb for us. For God to complete this final reconciliation, Jesus had to absorb the sin of the world. Due to God's hatred of sin, God had to look upon Jesus at some point while He hung on the cross as sin (past, present, and future). Thus,

I believe that when Christ cried out this plea, He had lost momentary contact with God, who temporarily broke off His connection with His Son who now had absorbed man's sin and perhaps had become sin, for that moment. Apparently He died shortly thereafter, uttering His final words: "It is finished" (John 19:30 NLT), and then "'Father, I entrust my spirit into your hands!' And with those words He breathed His last" (Luke, 23:46 NLT).

As a result, sin's grip on God's children loosened, and sin lost its sting and control over the lives of those who have accepted Christ's sacrifice and resurrection as a surrogate for their sins past, present, and future. His sacrifice provides forgiveness as long as we remain faithful to Him as our Lord and Savior. For this reason, Jesus came to earth, and for this reason, accepting this sacrifice can be the greatest leap of your life. This powerful fact of God's love for Christ and us is where we start in response to the question a few pages back: "Where and how can we find help and guidance as a result of Christ's life here on earth?"

Finding Help in Components of God's Plan

The answer to that question appears in the final few pages of this chapter. Two important considerations to keep in mind in this regard are the following. First, God and Christ love us far more than we are capable of imagining. Secondly, They also understand our susceptibility to temptation and sin. Therefore, an important part of God's plan for our salvation is that Christ's life here on earth should produce a strong and lasting effect on His children forever and provide the ongoing support for our faith in Him during our lifetimes. Thus He offered to become our Lord and Savior. He set an example with His life on how we should strive to live our lives. He demonstrated a passion for the Temple (God's House) as a forerunner of how the church would become so important to the growth of Christians and Christianity. And finally, He offered, through the Holy Spirit, to be with us all during our lifetimes, promising never to abandon us here on earth and to welcome us to eternal life with Him following our deaths.

Jesus Came to Become Our Lord and Savior

First, we must accept the truth that Jesus came down to earth to teach us, die on the cross as a substitute for our past, present, and future sins, and rise from the dead so that we might have life eternal. The following five short passages are among many that support the purpose of Christ's life here on earth.

> "For he hath made him to be sin for us, who knew no sin; that we might be made the righteousness of God in him" (2 Corinthians 5:21 KJV).

> "Who his own self bare our sins in his own body on the tree" (1 Peter 2:24 KJV).

> "I am the way, the truth, and the life; no man cometh unto the Father but by me" (John 14:6 KJV).

> "Verily, verily, I say unto you, He that heareth my word, and believeth on him that sent me, hath everlasting life, and shall not come into condemnation; but is passed from death unto life" (John 5:24 KJV).

> "There is therefore now no condemnation to them which are in Christ Jesus" (Romans 8:1 KJV).

Accepting this truth, establishing daily prayer, and growing in your trust and faith in Christ are the very first steps to a more abundant life spiritually here on earth and life eternal after death. How could this decision not be the greatest leap of your life!

This genuine faith and trust, along with Christ's teachings, will give you the foundation upon which you can live your life with joy and peace, patterned after the standard Christ established here on earth. Yes, we will still sin, and we will from time to time stumble. But if we are faithful in our acceptance of Christ as our Savior and Lord, daily strengthened through prayer and fellowship with God, and dependent on the power of the Holy Spirit (discussed in Chapter IV), we will become very capable of having sin become the exception rather than the practice in our lives.

Jesus Had to Set the Example

Jesus led this perfect life while facing all of the temptations and obstacles that we face throughout our lives. He did so to set an example with a high bar for us to strive to reach in the way we live our own lives. We can grab hold of the important teachings and pronouncements He gave us that guide us on how we can best strive to reach this standard. He knows, too, the nature of man and the temptations of life that

The Greatest Leap of Your Life

can lead man away from believing the spiritual truth He has taught. So Christ sent the Holy Spirit to guide and strengthen us. The Holy Spirit is another major answer to the question: "Where and how can we find help?" The Holy Spirit is the subject of the next chapter.

Mankind was much the same two thousand years ago as we are today. I believe that God carefully conceived Christ's three-year ministry to maximize its impact on both those alive at the time and all of us that lived after Christ's life, death, and resurrection. One particular example of the former is the circumstances and timing of Lazarus's death and the powerful impact this event had on the people at the time this miracle occurred.

> A man named Lazarus was sick. He lived in Bethany with his sisters, Mary and Martha. This is the Mary who poured the expensive perfume on the Lord's feet and wiped them with her hair. Her brother, Lazarus, was sick. So the two sisters sent a message to Jesus telling him, "Lord, the one you love is very sick."
> But when Jesus heard about it he said, "Lazarus's sickness will not end in death. No, it is for the glory of God. I, the Son of God, will receive glory from this." Although Jesus loved Martha, Mary, and Lazarus, he stayed where he was for the next two days and did not go to them. Finally after two days, he said to his disciples, "Let's go to Judea again."

But his disciples objected. "Teacher," they said, "only a few days ago the Jewish leaders in Judea were trying to kill you." ...

Then he told them plainly, "Lazarus is dead. And for your sake, I am glad I wasn't there, because this will give you another opportunity to believe in me. Come, let's go see him." ...

When Jesus arrived He approached Martha ... Jesus told her, "Your brother will rise again ... I am the resurrection and the life. Those who believe in me, even though they die like everyone else, will live again. They are given eternal life for believing in me and will never perish. Do you believe this, Martha?"

"Yes, Lord," she told him.

Jesus responded, "Didn't I tell you that you will see God's glory if you believe?" So they rolled the stone aside. Then Jesus looked up to heaven and said, "Father, thank you for hearing me. You always hear me, but I said it out loud for the sake of all these people standing here, so they will believe you sent me." Then Jesus shouted, "Lazarus, come out!" And Lazarus came out, bound in graveclothes, his face wrapped in a headcloth. Jesus told them, "Unwrap him and let him go!"

John 11:1–8, 14, 23, 25-27, 40-44 NLT

Many of the people who were with Mary believed in Jesus when they saw this happen. But some went to the Pharisees and told them what Jesus had done. Then the leading priests and Pharisees called the high council together to discuss the situation. "What are we going to do?" they asked each other. "This man certainly performs many miraculous signs. If we leave him alone, the whole nation will follow him, and then the Roman army will come and destroy both our Temple and our nation."

And one of them, Caiaphas, who was high priest that year, said, "How can you be so stupid? Why should the whole nation be destroyed? Let this one man die for the people."

This prophecy that Jesus should die for the entire nation came from Caiaphas in his position as high priest. He didn't think of it himself; he was inspired to say it. It was a prediction that Jesus' death would be not for Israel only, but for the gathering together of all the children of God scattered around the world.

So from that time on the Jewish leaders began to plot Jesus' death.

John 11:45–54 NLT

This particular miracle may have had more impact on the people at the time than any other that Jesus performed. It preceded His triumphant entry into Jerusalem just prior to His crucifixion. It also was a major catalyst for the scribes to hasten Christ's crucifixion within days.

Jesus set the example of how to live a sin-free life as a standard for us to strive to attain. His mind and life were filled with love, compassion, patience, faith, mercy, gentleness, and forgiveness. God knows that we are not capable of being perfect and that sin will remain a problem for mankind. But now, because of the perfect life and sacrifice of Christ, we can strive to live our lives better and walk away from slavery to the habit of sin. However, we need help to gain our freedom.

Focus on the Importance of God's House – the Church

One of Christ's strong passions here on earth, expressed for our benefit, was His love for His Father's house (temple, church), and he related it to the mission of His life here on earth in John 2:13–25 NLT:

> It was time for the annual Passover celebration, and Jesus went to Jerusalem. In the Temple area he saw merchants selling cattle, sheep, and doves for sacrifices; and he saw money changers behind their counters. Jesus made a whip from some ropes and chased them all out of the Temple. He drove out the sheep and oxen, scattered the money changers' coins over the floor, and turned over their tables. Then, going over to the people who sold doves, he told them, "Get these things out of here. Don't turn my Father's house into a marketplace!"
> Then his disciples remembered this prophecy from the Scriptures: "Passion for God's house burns within me."
> "What right do you have to do these things?" the Jewish leaders demanded. "If you have this authority from God, show us a miraculous sign to prove it."
> "All right," Jesus replied. "Destroy this temple, and in three days I will raise it up."

"What!" they exclaimed. "It took forty-six years to build this Temple, and you can do it in three days?" But by "this temple," Jesus meant his body. After he was raised from the dead, the disciples remembered that he had said this. And they believed both Jesus and the Scriptures.

Because of the miraculous signs he did in Jerusalem at the Passover celebration, many people were convinced that he was indeed the Messiah. But Jesus didn't trust them, because he knew what people were really like. No one needed to tell him about human nature.

I insert this passage because it seems to me that one of Christ's messages to us was that He loved the "temple" (church) because as the house of God it provided a venue for fellow worshipers to praise their God and support one another in their faith, share their lives, and nurture the lives of others. Because those there had defiled that purpose, Jesus was angry that the temple had been turned into a marketplace. I believe that God and Christ knew that the church was to become an important place for His children to find answers and support during the course of their lives and their spiritual growth. It has been a focal point for the growth of Christianity and Christians for the past two thousand years.

Jesus Gives Us Our Helper

Christ came to earth to help us with our struggles because of God's great love for us. But as strong as God's love is for us, His hate for sin is just as strong. Therefore, God had to reconcile His love and justice with the sin of man. The only way to reconcile God's hatred of sin with His love for His children was to sacrifice His Son at the cross as a substitute for our sins. This necessity is so important to grasp. It is the sole reason why a righteous God can forgive the sin which He hates so much. He can forgive what He hates because His Son, whom He loved beyond measure, justified us, gaining His Father's forgiveness through His death on the cross.

> For God so loved the world, that He gave his only begotten son, that whosoever believeth in Him, should not perish, but have everlasting life. For God sent not his Son into the world to condemn the world; but that the world through him might be saved (John 3:16-17 KJV).

It's very important to know that Christ did not abandon us some two thousand years ago. He said: "Fear not, for I will be with you always." Jesus said after His resurrection:

"When I depart to my Heavenly Father I will send you the Comforter – the Holy Spirit."

> Quite clearly Jesus did not say that His death on the cross would mark the cessation of His ministry. The night before His death He repeatedly told the disciples that He would send the Holy Spirit.
> The night before He was to die, He told His disciples, "It is expedient for you that I go away: for if I go not away, the Comforter will not come unto you; but if I depart, I will send him unto you" (John 16:7). Before He could send the Holy Spirit, who is the Comforter, Jesus had to go away: first, to the death of the cross, then to the resurrection; then to the ascension into heaven. Only then could He send the Holy Spirit on the day of Pentecost.
> *The Mind of Christ*, T. W. Hunt

An important part of the Good News that must never be lost is that God wants us to find happiness and security here on earth as well as in heaven with Him. Christ died for our sins not only so that we might have life eternal but so that we might have life more abundantly here on earth. How does He do so?

Well, believers have every reason to be upbeat in life because Christ has overcome death, and though we all will physically die someday, we will be alive spiritually forever. We can live life in paradise with God following our physical death here on earth. In addition, the believer has enhanced security and faith in this life because the Holy Spirit gives all believers the guidance and strength to live better, more positive, and more loving lives here on earth. This real help creates optimism about dealing with life's challenges and problems in a manner that brings greater confidence, excitement, and anticipation to living each day.

The Holy Spirit is not imaginary. He is real, and He is the Spirit of God. He is alive within us, and as our relationship with the Holy Spirit grows, it reinforces the truth of Christ, changes our outlook and approach to life, and strengthens our faith, enabling us to live better, more confident, peaceful, and joy-filled lives. How can you not be upbeat or optimistic about life when your faith accepts and feels the above as an absolute truth?

Jesus came to earth to save us in God's plan for our salvation. For me personally, I have found the strength, peace, and a positive outlook on life, which are all inherent in my acceptance of Christ as my Savior and Lord. When I took this greatest leap of my life, the Holy Spirit took up a presence in my soul. His constant presence is a part of Christ's promise for a more abundant life here on earth and is another major blessing that is ours because Jesus came to earth for us.

This leap of faith in accepting the purpose of Christ's life here on earth is very important. When one accepts this purpose, he has begun a new and exciting journey in life. It's important, however, to know that you don't have to travel it alone. You will have great strength and guidance to help you through the Holy Spirit, which is the focus of the next chapter.

Chapter V

The Holy Spirit - The Bridge for Your Leap

Theologians have studied, debated, and written about the Trinity of God the Father, the Lord Jesus Christ, and the Holy Spirit for centuries. What does the construct mean? How do the distinct Persons all relate? What is the ongoing relationship of the separate entities which are the single Deity that the Trinity represents and is?

The complexity and degree of interpretation involved in this analysis must be extensive. Obviously, an untrained individual like me has no business pretending to understand all there is to know about the theology of the Trinity.

But I'm undaunted by this mystery. Life is filled with uncertainties and the unknown, and that mysterious nature is why we must make a number of leaps in life. No individual in history has ever known everything there is to know about an individual subject, let alone the exhaustive catalogue of other subjects in life. However, to be knowledgeable and to attempt to learn about life, particularly things that are of most interest and/or priorities in our lives, is certainly good and important. And that thirst for knowledge, among other things, has led to the development of a significant number of people in life gaining expertise in certain subject matters which can enlighten us all. But even these experts are limited to the extent of knowledge they obtain in their lifetimes.

Part of what makes life so interesting and challenging is trying to sort out for ourselves the answers to questions, situations, problems, and challenges that are part of our everyday existence. As we make our way through the mysteries of life, it's interesting to learn from those who have general expertise in certain fields. The amount of time each of us devotes to these questions or mysteries varies by individual and by subject matter. In the end, we try to find an effective way or method of determining answers to matters in life that we believe are true or, at the very least, comfortable to us for whatever reason or reasons we may have. I guess this long-winded explanation states why I'm comfortable with my simplistic understanding of the complexity of the Trinity.

Why the Trinity – God, Jesus, and the Holy Spirit

God

I suppose that a logical question might be: If God wants us to believe, trust, and worship Him, why does He complicate this response by creating the complexity of the Trinity? Well, what I'm about to say about this matter is not based on scholarly study or research of theologians' writings. It is based on my own reasoning and faith developed over fifty years beginning at age thirteen. In order to understand the Holy Spirit better, let's first look at the first two persons of the Trinity: God and Jesus Christ.

The infinity of God is so unfathomable to our finite minds that, for many, the following may seem implausible. I believe that, when God created the world, He knew He would come down to earth in the form of God-man as Jesus Christ. He also knew that He would come into the hearts and souls of His children, who accepted Jesus as Lord and Savior, in the form of the Holy Spirit.

He knew that someday He would create humankind in His own image and that He would give humans a free will to choose their way in life. While He loves all His creations, He provided this free will for humanity because we are the greatest and most precious of all His creations. His desire to be loved and worshiped required a genuine, real, directional love that must come from a free will rather than a robotic, automatic, or manufactured emotion.

He also knew that the world He created would develop imperfections, temptations, and distractions, because of the inherent sin that exists in imperfect, finite mankind and the world he inhabits. Sin, as defined in my handy Funk and Wagnalls, is: "1) A transgression, esp., when deliberate, of a law having divine authority." That entry is not terribly definitive, but trying to define sin comprehensively is not my objective.

God, through the influence of the Holy Spirit upon certain selected individuals, guided the writings of the Bible in the Old and New Testaments. From the beginning, God established in these documents His standards for living our lives. And from the beginning, mankind has fallen far short of the perfect performance.

I believe that God understands and accepts imperfect performance, but He does not accept a mediocre effort to strive for the standard He has established. I must admit that the previous statement is an oversimplification and one that I know doesn't fully describe God's expectations of us, as He will not compromise certain truths. I say so, perhaps, to encourage myself and others, that we not be discouraged with our imperfections and shortcomings along the way. As long as we keep working toward growth in our love, trust, and faith in our Father in heaven, our Lord and Savior Jesus Christ, and the Holy Spirit and truly repenting when we have sinned knowingly, we will find comfort and strength to continue our important journey with Him, despite our sins and the obstacles we face.

Jesus Christ

In God's great plan of salvation for His children, He knew some two thousand years ago that the time had arrived for Him to come to earth in the form of His only begotten Son, Jesus Christ.

Because His children were still struggling with their lives and their faith, God knew that man required a more direct proof of His love, compassion, and expectations, as well as a very clear requirement for salvation and eternal life with Him. Through witnesses and writings from those influenced by the Holy Spirit, the New Testament has documented Jesus' life very well. The Gospels are filled with His teachings and parables and the examples of His living, thinking, healing, and other miraculous acts that attest to His existence. His life, death, and the resurrection of His body and spirit are part of God's plan, in which He overcame permanent death for all of us who believe. The Gospels provide evidence of the sacrifice that He died in place of our sins, that those who believe in the resurrection will not perish, and that we, too, shall rise and have life eternal with Him in His paradise following our own earthly death. The New Testament of the Holy Bible documents all of these truths.

Jesus said: "Abide in Me, and I in you. As the branch cannot bear fruit of itself, unless it abides in the vine, so neither can you, unless you abide in Me. I am the vine, you are the branches; he who abides in Me, and I in him, he bears much fruit; for apart from Me you can do nothing" (John 15:4, 5 KJV). In abiding in Him through faith and prayer, we are better able to face the struggles, challenges, and opportunities of life.

As powerful as Jesus' life, teachings, sacrifice, and resurrection were, God and Jesus knew that we finite and imperfect beings would need an ongoing presence of strength in order to live our lives as Jesus taught us to live them. That strength is the Holy Spirit. Once you have taken the greatest of all leaps in accepting the truth, love, sacrifice, and resurrection of Jesus Christ, the Holy Spirit comes to reside in your very being to guide and strengthen you.

The Holy Spirit

Jesus said that He would never leave us. His promise is true, as God and Christ sent the Holy Spirit for the purpose of living within our souls to give us guidance, strength, and a sense of peace and joy. The Holy Spirit entered the hearts and souls of the apostles on Pentecost, the fiftieth day following Christ's resurrection, and brought to them an incredible strength, direction, insight, and power to begin the long journey of spreading the truth of Christ. Relatively few people in the world at that time accepted the truth of Christ, but through the power of the Holy Spirit, the apostles began what became an incredible growth and influence of Christianity over the next two thousand years. And many of them were executed for their faith and works in Christ. The way that Christianity has grown from these humble beginnings is truly astounding. The power of the Holy Spirit truly has been at work in enabling Christianity to grow over the past twenty centuries to its present influence in the world today.

Jesus Christ knew well the weakness of man, as well as man's need to know that He, as our Savior and Lord, would never abandon us. However, He needed to accomplish His work here on earth before He could give us that help. During His life and ministry here on earth, Jesus referred to the absolute importance and promise of this help through the Holy Spirit.

Here are just a few of Jesus' many references in Scripture to the Holy Spirit:

> "And I will pray the Father, and he shall give you another Comforter, that he may abide with you for ever; Even the Spirit of truth; whom the world cannot receive, because it seeth him not, neither knoweth him; but ye know him; for he dwelleth with you, and shall be in you" (John 14:16–17 KJV).

> "But when the Comforter is come, whom I will send unto you from the Father, even the Spirit of truth, which proceedeth from the Father, he shall testify of me" (John 15:26 KJV).

"When the Spirit of truth comes, he will guide you into all truth" (John 16:13 NLT).

References to the Holy Spirit appear in many sections of the Bible describing His impact upon our lives, which is to provide incredible insight into the simple and complex things of our spiritual lives and to assist significantly in helping us interpret more clearly the message of God and Christ written in the Bible.

The Holy Spirit is in every way equal to God and Jesus Christ as part of the Trinity. He is God, and He resides in all believers to guide, enlighten, convict, strengthen, and provide joy and peace in their hearts and souls. As we Christians grow stronger in our faith, He becomes a larger influence in developing our understanding of God's expectations and truth. He guides us in our development and enlightenment. He becomes a part of our conscience to guide us in dealing with all the challenges, temptations, and hurdles in life. He provides insight into understanding better the written Word and the circumstances that we face in life. The Holy Spirit is very real to believers because of the strength, peace, and insight He brings to them personally. This ongoing relationship only reinforces the truth to the believer that the all-powerful, infinite Supreme Being, God, sent His Son to die for us and also sent the Holy Spirit to those who believe following Christ's resurrection.

The Holy Spirit takes up residence within each believer to provide an ongoing, ever-present source of strength with which to live our lives in faith, trust, and surrender to the truth of Jesus Christ. For the rest of our lives, the Holy Spirit lives inside each of us who believes. Imagine that! Accept that.

An Uplifting Experience with the Holy Spirit

I personally have felt the guidance and strength of the Holy Spirit in my life many, many times. One of the most difficult periods of my life and tenure of nearly thirty years as a hospital CEO came in the early nineties, when I had my only real, serious division with the medical staff, which engendered significant opposition. In this story, you will see that much was at stake for me and my family and that the presence of the Holy Spirit in my life during this episode was significant in how I handled the situation and its outcome.

By way of background, I arrived at this modest-sized community hospital in 1978 as the thirty-four-year-old CEO.

Obviously, I knew that I was green behind the ears to some extent, and I wanted to be sure that I got off on the right foot. I heeded some advice early on that I had best get to know immediately and develop a good working relationship with a very influential MD. I did so. Within days, I invited him to my office in order to gain his perspective on the hospital (which was in a very fragile condition when I arrived) and to learn more about his outlook on the direction for the hospital and his assessment of the community we served. This initial contact worked well for both of us at the outset. We developed an open dialogue, and my comfort level was such that within several months I even selected him as my personal doctor.

As time progressed and I became more familiar with the issues and priorities which informed the direction I believed the hospital needed to take, the relationship slowly began to unravel. I found this doctor to be someone who didn't like to hear the word "no." And as the differences of opinion began to grow and accumulate, so did the breakdown in communication. Evidently, this individual was something of a "street fighter" or "corridor organizer", as I and my colleagues might term him. And so from about 1980 to the incident in the early nineties, I always knew that he was in the background, stirring the pot. Despite his influence with some of the staff, his behavior was never a really big deal, but it remained annoying and periodically disruptive, nonetheless.

In the early 1990s, this doctor had befriended another member of the staff who didn't like me and who was equally aggressive in the corridor politics. One day I had a confrontation with this particular individual, who had come to my office to complain about something. I don't remember the specific issue, but I knew that he and the previously mentioned doctor had been working behind the scenes with some others to get the medical staff to bring forward a vote of no confidence through one of their formal medical staff meetings. While that vote never happened, the time surrounding it was very contentious, because the ringleaders were speaking of this discord out in the public, at the nursing stations, and even to the press. During this same period of time, my father in Florida became very sick with prostate cancer and died in November 1991. My mother, who moved up to live with our family in February 1992, died the very next month. Needless to say, this period of time was filled with stress and sadness.

The majority of medical doctors on staff clearly did not partake in the revolt. In fact, many MDs were organizing in support of me. A few contentious months later, the hospital held a joint conference committee meeting (executive committee of the board and executive committee of the staff) and talked over the problem. Those who were against me didn't like the outcome. However, directly following this meeting, I met with the chairman of the board and a few members of the board in my office. Despite the strong support given me at this meeting and throughout this ordeal, I offered to resign, because I didn't want the very deep bitterness of a relentless few to become a cancer in the organization. My offer was sincere, but the board members refused and remained very adamant in their support.

But I wasn't out of the woods yet, as the vocal minority was still angry and strategizing for their final opportunity to get the CEO at the upcoming annual meeting. Expecting a larger turnout than normal, the hospital reserved the large conference hall at the Kimberly Clark plant located in town. The annual meeting, unless a controversy is brewing, usually attracts only forty or so people. This time, because of the conflict that some members of the medical staff had made public, the planners anticipated more. The turnout that day was more than a hundred people.

Five or six of the doctors who stalwartly opposed me attended the meeting. As required by the bylaws, the agenda called for the chairman's report, the president's report, which includes the financial status of the hospital, and an invitation to attendees to ask questions or make comments, among other items.

For the preceding fourteen years of my employment, probably a total of three or four people asked questions or made comments at these meetings. The hospital administration knew that this year would be different. This day was tense for many of us, including the chairman and me. The press always covered the event, and we hoped that this meeting would not turn out to create a lot of bad publicity for the hospital, which would erode its strong support within the community. In a smaller community, bad press can have a much more damaging impact on an institution than it does in a more urban setting.

Just as the meeting was about to start, my chairman turned to me and said, "I'm not up to giving my report today; I'm going to start by going directly to you and your report." I was quite surprised, because this individual was a solid professional and a good chairman. But the pressure of the day got to him, as such pressure can and does affect all of us. While I had my moments of apprehension before the meeting and while traveling across town, I knew that

The Greatest Leap of Your Life

the Holy Spirit had strengthened me for the task, despite the risk of embarrassment that could fall on me and the hospital when the members of the medical staff had the opportunity to speak. I got to the podium and spoke with great confidence and assurance as I reviewed for the audience the results of the past year and the top priorities for the upcoming year. That speech was perhaps one of my strongest presentations, and I know that the audience received it well. Whether my words mitigated to some extent the response of the MDs in attendance, I don't know. However, the chairman and I responded to the questions raised in such an effective manner that the press reports the next day about the hospital's annual meeting were very positive. The tension calmed quickly after that day, and my positive relationships with the medical staff resumed and remained strong and positive for the rest of my tenure as well.

I think you can imagine the pressure on any one of us of this kind of situation, where employment may be on the line. The pressure created by just a few very motivated MDs was intense and ongoing. My children at the time were seventeen, sixteen, and nine. My two daughters were obviously nearly college age, certainly not the best of times to have my job threatened. What clearly strengthened me during this ordeal was the power and guidance of the Holy Spirit. During the course of this process, I clearly remember Bob Sommer, my VP for human resources, looking deeply into my eyes at one point and saying, "Dick, I don't know how you do it." He was talking about my handling all this pressure with what he felt was incredible composure. I told him that I did so only because of my strong faith in something far greater than myself. The Holy Spirit is and was meant to be an incredible force in our lives. After all, the Holy Spirit is God, and He resides within every believer. Our faith in this power and love can give us strength for anything, literally reducing mountains to molehills as we face whatever is before us.

The Holy Spirit Is Ever Present

The power and peace of God the Holy Spirit living in you every moment of your life is what Jesus meant when He said that He would never abandon us, but would be with us always.

John Wesley, the founder of the Methodist denomination, spoke as follows to the power of the Holy Spirit:

It is hard to find words in the language of men, to explain the deep things of God. Indeed, there are none that will adequately express what the Spirit of God works in His children. But ... by the testimony of the Spirit, I mean, an inward impression on the soul, whereby the Spirit of God immediately and directly witnesses to my spirit, that I am a child of God; that Jesus Christ hath loved me, and given Himself for me; that all my sins are blotted out, and I, even I, am reconciled to God.

Wesley describes the strength, power, guidance, security, and love that Christ promised us by telling us that He would send the "Comforter," the Holy Spirit, to give us the guidance, strength, and insight to live our lives in faith, trust, and surrender to God's will and love for us. The Holy Spirit empowers us to have life more abundantly here on earth as well as life eternal through Jesus Christ. The Bible instructs us to "be filled with the Spirit" (Ephesians 5:18 KJV). When filled with the Spirit, you will produce the fruit of "love, joy, peace, long-suffering, gentleness, goodness, faith, meekness, temperance" (Galatians 5:22-23 KJV). I can assure you that these words are neither idle nor meaningless. They are the truth. A believer can and will find, believe, and firmly grasp a more satisfying life founded on a Rock, which grants him a security and peace that he has never felt before.

The Greatest Leap of Your Life

In concluding this chapter, I include the following excerpt from the book *Unto the Hills* by Billy Graham, along with a brief commentary on it.

> God the Holy Spirit is equal with the Son and with the Father in every respect. The Bible teaches that He is co-equal with God the Father and co-equal with God the Son. The Bible also teaches that the Holy Spirit is a Person. He is never to be referred to as "it." He is not just an agent; He is not just an influence. He is a mighty Person, the Holy Spirit of God.
>
> The Bible tells us that He is omnipotent. That means that He has all power.
>
> The Bible tells us that He is omnipresent. That means that He is everywhere at the same time.
>
> The Bible tells us that He is omniscient. That means that He has all knowledge. He knows everything that we do—He watches us. "His eye is on the sparrow," and if God the Spirit is watching the sparrow, how much more He is watching us every moment.
>
> He sees the thoughts and intents of our hearts. He delves into our minds, into the things we think, into the intents of our souls. He knows all about us. He knows everything ...
>
> The Bible teaches that the Holy Spirit is eternal. The Bible tells us that He is holy. He is referred to in the New Testament alone one hundred times as the Holy Spirit—absolute holiness, absolute purity, absolute righteousness.
>
> What should this mean to me? With the seventeenth century Anglican bishop, Jeremy Taylor, I can

say, "It is impossible for that man to despair who remembers that his Helper is omnipotent."

While I consider this passage to be an excellent and concise statement of fact about the Holy Spirit as I know Him, I also recognize that these words and Scripture can be glazed-eye words and concepts to many. What I mean is that both this statement and Scripture can seem surreal and therefore easily dismissible. They can appear to the reader as fantasy or a form of feel-good escapism.

What I offer to mitigate that image is a major thesis of this book, which I proposed that you accept earlier: God is infinite, and we are finite. As long as we look upon God, Jesus Christ, and the Holy Spirit under the human microscope with its inherent finiteness, we will forever resist taking the leap into the assurance that something far greater than mankind exists in our world: the unmatchable and infinite power, love, and forgiveness of God our Father, who has created His plan for our salvation. The exclamation point of God's great gift to us is the awesome power of the Holy Spirit to guide and strengthen all believers throughout the rest of their lives.

If and when you have arrived at this point, you have just taken the greatest leap of your life, and you have now begun a journey of great peace and joy that you have never experienced before! The work of the Holy Spirit in your soul reinforces what you have just accepted and provides over time new insights into God's plan for you and your life. During this process, believers become stronger in their faith and trust in their infinite God and their Lord and Savior Jesus Christ.

You have now been born again because of your leap, and the next chapter focuses on what that new birth means and its impact on your life going forward.

Chapter VI

Born Again - The Process That Sustains Your Leap

Exactly what is meant by "born again"? Perhaps the best known reference to this term in the Bible comes from a conversation between Nicodemus and Jesus.

Nicodemus, a Pharisee, was a highly esteemed man of God. He was a very learned man who had been drawn to Jesus and wanted to learn more from Him. He did so quietly, however, as the powerful Pharisees, as a group, both disdained and feared Jesus. During a conversation one night, Jesus responded to a question from Nicodemus as follows (John 3:3-7 RSV).

"Truly, truly, I say to you, unless one is born anew, he cannot see the Kingdom of God." Nicodemus said to Him, "How can a man be born when he is old? Can he enter a second time into his mother's womb and be born?" Jesus answered, "Truly, truly, I say to you, unless one is born of water and Spirit, he cannot enter the Kingdom of God. That which is born of flesh is flesh, and that which is born of the Spirit is spirit. Do not marvel that I said to you, you must be born anew."

We all hear the term "born-again Christians" used almost as if born-again Christians are somehow different than just plain Christians. Realistically, perhaps that assumption is so, but theoretically, no distinction should exist.

In its simplest yet most profound terms, a Christian is one who believes and accepts Jesus Christ as Lord and Savior, affirming that Jesus is the Son of God who came to earth as God-man to teach us how to live a better, less sinful life, to die on the cross as an atonement for the sins of each one of us who believes in Him, and to rise from the dead to demonstrate the reality of life eternal with Him in heaven, following our own earthly deaths.

When this true acceptance enters our hearts, minds, and souls, the Holy Spirit comes into our lives and enables us to begin to live a significantly different life. This process is called being born again. God has changed our minds about sin, and our priorities will now rest on a new foundation. Sin no longer will have dominion over you, as the old self begins to die, making way for a vibrant, new self.

A remarkable transformation occurs when this acceptance becomes genuine and the Holy Spirit comes into your life to guide and strengthen you to become a better, stronger, more faithful person who desires to live your life each day for your Lord and Savior. In so doing, you will find that your other relationships will blossom as well. In all of this change, a whole new peace and enthusiasm comes to your life that brings more joy than you have ever felt before. This explanation is the simplest one I can give for what is meant by the words "born again."

I sense that everyone who is truly born again experiences different degrees of emotion in terms of intensity and the time necessary for the transformation to sink or settle into day-to-day life. Either immediately or eventually, a new Christian begins to develop consistency in living daily life that is different than before. When and how this development occurs in each of our lives is probably as different as we human beings are different from one another.

The Greatest Leap of Your Life

Born Again – My Experience

As for me, my experience is so long ago that the detailed track I followed as a born again believer is not as clear as I would like. But here is something of what I do remember.

I grew up in a working-class community in Endicott, New York, in a wonderful neighborhood where the houses were right on top of one another, with nice little backyards, a ball field down at the end of the street, and a public golf course bordering our neighborhood. We moved to this community in 1949, when I was approximately five years old. We lived next door to the Hosays, who had a seven-year-old boy named Joseph and twin girls, Jean and Jane, who were maybe two or three at the time.

Over time, Joe and I became the best of friends, despite our many differences. He loved the Brooklyn Dodgers, and I loved the New York Yankees. He was a big fan of Roy Campanella, Jackie Robinson, and Pee Wee Reese, and I was the biggest Mickey Mantle fan in the world – or so I thought, anyway. Joe loved Notre Dame, which I hated (although I do root for them now), and I was a big fan of Bud Wilkinson's Oklahoma Sooners (an affinity which was initially influenced by the fact that Mickey Mantle was born in Oklahoma.) Joe was an accomplished musician, an outstanding professional accordionist, but I had failed miserably at piano lessons. He was a high honor student who was considering both medicine and the priesthood while in high school. I was a mediocre student at best who didn't like to focus as much as I should have on my homework assignments, and my distraction showed. All I wanted to do was to become a major league baseball player.

Joe Hosay was also a wonderfully decent, considerate, mature young man during his early teens. He didn't swear, and he treated all people with respect. He was truly a young adolescent to emulate, while I was a hothead who swore a lot and didn't come close to measuring up to my friend. But the two things we had in common were our love for sports, particularly baseball, and our friendship. Joe was an all-star catcher who was considered at age fifteen to have some real possibilities for professional baseball when he finished school. We competed with one another, and perhaps that intensity, competition, and love for one another made us both better players. Interestingly, we actually had a third item in common. Our girl friends were sisters, Carol and Linda Snow, the "knockouts" in our respective classes, if I do say so myself.

The Greatest Leap of Your Life

Despite my lack of maturity, I loved and admired Joe and can never remember being jealous of him in any way. We shared a happy childhood together.

Right around the first of July, 1957, my dad and I drove Joe and his mother to the doctor's office, as Joe had not been feeling well for a few days. His dad was working and had taken their only car, and my dad was on vacation. Joe was hospitalized that day, and before the month was out, he died on July 30, 1957, at age fifteen from a very rare condition that was ultimately written up in one of the medical journals.

I was stunned and nearly overwhelmed with a sense of confusion and loss. I can remember for the first time wondering what this world was all about. *How does something like this happen? This is it? I don't see Joe again ever?* I'll never forget the next day or two after his death, when my dad had the afternoon Yankees game on the radio. I heard Mel Allen's voice announcing the game, and Bob Turley, my favorite pitcher at the time, was pitching that day. I kept asking myself: *How can Mel Allen even think of announcing, or Bob Turley even consider pitching a game today, when my best friend Joe has just died? Don't they understand that this day is too sad to be playing baseball?* That troubling and mournful thought is as clear to me today as it was back then.

The Greatest Leap of Your Life

I was one of six pallbearers for Joe's funeral, and I'll never forget walking his casket back up the aisle following the service at St. Joseph's Church, and fighting so hard to not start bawling out loud. I recall Linda and Carol sitting in the pews doing just that as we proceeded toward the back of the church. I couldn't wait to get back to the car, out of view, so that I could let the tears fall freely.

The next difficult thing for me to face that day was returning to Joe's house with family and close friends. I thought that I would find tremendous grief and a very sad atmosphere. What I found was much different than what I expected. While everyone there loved and missed Joe dearly, the atmosphere was noisy with laughter and people seemingly enjoying each other's company. That joy and laughter upset me; I couldn't get joyful about anything that day or for a period of time afterwards. What I didn't realize at the time was that this gathering was in no way disrespectful. Instead, it was meant to be a happy and respectful celebration of Joe's new place of peace with his God and his Savior. At the time, I just didn't understand or like what I saw.

As the days, weeks, and months passed, somehow, some way, God got my attention. I don't remember how soon after Joe's death I began to be led to God and Christ.

The Greatest Leap of Your Life

I do remember that the process didn't begin overnight, yet I do believe that within several months I came to know and accept Jesus Christ as my Savior.

You know that we all have a number of regrets in our life. Well, looking back, a regret I have from my childhood is that I didn't work at my piano lessons. I've wished many times that I could sit down at the keyboard and play beautiful music like Joe did with his accordion. I also regret that I didn't have some sort of diary to record my transition to being born again. It certainly would have helped in the writing of this book. Nonetheless, here is what I do remember.

What is very clear is that Billy Graham's influence was a significant part of how I came to my new awareness of God, Christ, and faith. I can remember lying in bed on Sunday nights at 10 p.m. when *The Hour of Decision* with Billy Graham would come on the radio in my parents' room and reach into my room, which was right across the hall. I didn't fall asleep until he had finished his fifteen-to-twenty-minute message.

As an aside about Mr. Graham, I do believe that God especially blessed him to deliver His message. This man possesses tremendous insight, delivery, and faith that have touched millions of people in their development as born-again Christians. He rightfully gives any such credit to God, Jesus, and the Holy Spirit, but I do believe that God uses His children as instruments to help the rest of us along in life. I believe that God selected Billy Graham to be a giant instrument within His plan. Of all the people in the world that I wish I could have met, he would have been the first.

I think that his success in reaching people had to do, in part, with the fact that he very consistently related the simple message of salvation that God has given us. He didn't make it complicated, yet he reinforced it differently each week with Scripture, examples, and/or anecdotes. He could put a complex subject matter into a consistent simplicity that got to the essence of God's message to us through Christ. As I said in Chapter I, despite the complexity of this world, there are true benefits to breaking down these complexities to simple pieces and applications for dealing with the reality of life. I certainly applied this principle in my forty years of experience in management. I believe that, when you can explain the core of what's important to your people, they will follow you, because they also understand it and believe in its importance to them and the organization of which they are a part.

The Greatest Leap of Your Life

Going back to recall some of my transition, I started with chronology to stimulate my memory. Joe Hosay died in the summer of 1957, and I entered the ninth grade approximately one month later. Our school included first through ninth grades; so we didn't enter our high school building (tenth to twelfth grades) until our sophomore year. I don't know that I had yet been born again while I attended school in the old building. I probably was in transition to understanding some profound truths about life and God and doing my best to absorb them.

A New Growth

I'm certain that God brought a new calm to my life as this transition progressed. I recall having wonderfully fun relationships that year with a lot of friends that I don't recall befriending to that degree earlier, other than Joe and a few others. I became far more interested in people and getting to know them and their interests rather than just being concerned about myself. For example, I recall having very interesting conversations with Bud Wallace, who sat across from me in homeroom, about his experiences playing football for the high school freshman team. He had to travel to the high

The Greatest Leap of Your Life

school at the end of the day for this opportunity. He was playing quarterback, and he described all the plays he had to learn and remember. I recall thinking how difficult that task must be and how much different than the sandlot football I knew. Bud was kind of a quiet, shy boy, but I knew that talking football brought him right out of his shell. I was interested in having Bud and others share with me what was important to them. That interest was a distinct change in me from who I used to be.

I recall having developed a great relationship, as well as a crush, with a new girl in town, Diane Poulton. She sat in front of me in homeroom, and we seemed to be able to talk about anything together. She was very pretty and personable. Even after she gently let me know that the feeling (crush) was not mutual, we continued to be great friends that year and through high school. Interestingly, I ended up playing high school football with her eventual husband, Dave Robinson.

This new interest in people was just the beginning of developing, with ease, a larger network of friends that I enjoyed. In this new transition, I genuinely wanted to know who they were and what was important to them. I was in the beginning stages of becoming a "new" person.

I had become more outgoing and far less aggressive. I was more at peace about virtually everything. Instead of getting into fights on the playground and being hauled into the principal's office, I spent time playing for the school's basketball team and singing in a special chorus group. I set aside Friday nights for going to the movies with friends. My approach to people and life clearly began a transition based on God somehow touching my mind and heart with new meanings to life that eventually culminated in my accepting Jesus Christ as my Lord and Savior and being born again. I found a new excitement to life and my relationships with friends and family. Every new day was exciting to me. If only I had chronicled this transformation when it happened, I could have related far more concerning this initial transition.

Once I accepted Jesus as my Lord and Savior, I began to mature as a Christian and as a human being. I went from a young kid who swore a lot and had a pretty tough temper to someone who had found a new peace and patience. I had adopted a higher standard by which to live. I remember clearly one day my sister Marlene saying to me, "You have the patience of Job." I'm sure she saw the incredible change that had come over my life.

The Greatest Leap of Your Life

I was now more focused on prayer and the growth and development it brought to me as a human being and Christian. I had become more respectful and considerate of my family, friends, and others. I cared more for people around me and wanted to be more helpful. I didn't think very much about what people thought about me. I primarily cared more about being faithful to God and my Savior and leaving everything else to take care of itself. I left worry to God and just trusted in Him to help me along in life. Instead of the fears that we all have in growing up, no matter what style of life we lead, the peace within me nullified these emotions for the most part. Life with Christ had become over time an exhilarating experience of steadiness and continued joy.

I was a new person, because much of my old self had died. However, I still loved sports. I played baseball and football in high school and freshman football and three years of varsity baseball in college. I even still thought I could play professional baseball. When I was in college, there were no Division I, II, and IIIs, and freshmen could not play varsity. My freshman year at Ithaca College, I was voted by my teammates as MVP of our baseball team. Meanwhile, the varsity went to the college World Series (one of only nine teams in the country), beating the University of Missouri before

The Greatest Leap of Your Life

being eliminated by losing by one run to both University of Texas and one of the California teams. I probably wouldn't have made the varsity even if freshmen were allowed, but that playoff was the closest I ever got to the big time! By the time I finished my senior year, the reality had set in — I was not going to become a major league baseball player!

In thinking back to high school, my teammates often called me "The Preacher," even though I was not aggressive at all with people in expressing my beliefs. But they saw a kid with a strong faith in something, a kid who somehow was special in his ability to relate to others. I truly had been born again, and I knew the most wonderful feeling in the world: understanding the great underpinning of this conversion. I relate my story primarily to demonstrate that being born again does not preclude anyone from continuing with most of the other good aspects of life that he always enjoyed as a kid or an adult.

Born Again – In Summary

There is so much that can be written and explained about "born again," but I'm not a theologian. Furthermore, I wish to remain as concise and direct as possible so that I keep the attention of others while I explain the simple but powerful basics of God's plan for our salvation. However, I will talk more about the born-again process in Chapter VII, as it is a fundamental piece of God's plan for our salvation.

In concluding this chapter on being born again, I have again been led to the following section from Billy Graham's *Unto the Hills*.

> Before He left His disciples, Christ promised that He would send a Comforter to help them in the trials, cares, and temptations of life. This word *comforter* means "one that helps alongside." He is the Holy Spirit, the powerful Third Person of the Trinity. The moment we are born again He takes up residence in our hearts.
>
> We may not emotionally feel Him there, but here again we must exercise faith. Believe it! Accept it as a fact of faith! He is in our hearts to help us in our Christian walk.
>
> We are told that He sheds the love of God abroad in our hearts. He produces the fruit of the Spirit: "love, joy, peace, long-suffering, gentleness, goodness, faith, meekness, temperance" (Galatians 5:22, 23). We cannot possibly manufacture this fruit in our own cannery. It is supernaturally manufactured by the Holy Spirit who lives in our hearts!
>
> I must yield to Him ... surrender to Him ... give Him control of my life. Through that surrender I will find happiness!

Being born again seems to have something of a mystery to it. Some say it can happen multiple times, while others say it can happen only once. Those who say it happens only once might acknowledge that there are reinforcement periods that take place in one's lifetime. I tend to believe it's the latter.

In either case, the Holy Spirit comes into our hearts when we are born again. The comfort and strength of this appearance when it happens is incredible and real. But the born-again Christian's work has only begun. We must work at this new relationship in a similar way to how we work at maintaining strong relationships with our marriages, families, and co-workers.

We maintain an edge or flow to our relationship with the Holy Spirit through praying, reading the Bible and other beneficial readings, and focusing on how we can live better lives for God in gratitude for His love and the sacrifice of His Son. We must exercise our minds in this process diligently and daily. Doing so keeps the Holy Spirit alive in our minds and souls and provides a staying power and endurance of faith that is not unlike the analogy of the staying power and endurance we can achieve through daily physical exercise.

Like physical exercise, spiritual diligence does not have to occur twenty-four hours a day. But the born-again endurance does require that the process take place on a daily basis so that the spiritual strength that comes from this relationship with the Holy Spirit remains fresh, vibrant, enduring, and a constant presence in our minds and souls. As we become consistent and remain strong in this effort, we more readily feel the presence of the Holy Spirit each day, and surprising new insights will come into our lives through this new relationship. The peace, security, and comfort from this ongoing relationship can be among the greatest gifts and strengths of life.

Just like the leap you took with your commitment to your marriage or your career selection, the born-again leap and process of refinement is one of continued effort, maturity and growth to keep it alive, vibrant, and well. In so doing, you develop and maintain great peace and joy in your life, benefits which form the focus of Chapter VII.

Chapter VII
Joy and Peace That Is Real

As covered previously, when we truly accept Jesus Christ into our hearts as Lord and Savior, we are born again, and the Holy Spirit takes up residence in our hearts and souls. I know that such assurance may sound like simplistic magic to many people, but it is consistent with God's plan for those who accept Christ and consistent with Jesus' message that He would not leave us alone but would send the Holy Spirit to reside within us for the rest of our lives.

The Holy Spirit is God. Because of your belief, He will reside in you to guide and strengthen you every day through your trust in this truth. The fruit of the Spirit, as noted in the previous chapter, is love, joy, peace, long-suffering, gentleness, goodness, faith, meekness, and temperance. These characteristics described the living Christ, and they can become your characteristics in this new relationship with the Holy Spirit. He will be your renewed conscience that will lead you in a different direction spiritually than you have ever experienced before. As you open your mind and heart to Him as a result of your great leap of acceptance, you will find a new presence in your soul that brings a refreshing peace and reassurance to you daily, as well as an optimism and enthusiasm for life that you have never felt before. You will feel a whole new sense of control as you surrender to Him your worries and anxieties.

When Does It Come?

It's important to know, however, that all of these benefits may not appear overnight. We are like little children learning to become adults as we increasingly exercise our new enlightenment through Christ and the Holy Spirit. We need to learn more through the Bible and its interpretations by learned individuals who have also been born again. Like young athletes who must exercise to stay in condition to perform, we must exercise our new gift through prayer and fellowship with God, seeking His strength, guidance, and insight into the wonderful truth of our salvation through Christ. The repetition of reaching out to God in prayer and reading the Bible on a daily basis strengthens us and provides more insight about God's plan of salvation and how we can enhance our service to Him.

Redundancy and Vince Lombardi

As noted in the Preface, this book is an effort to simplify what could be considered a complex subject. Considering this goal, the reader may come away with a sense of redundancy because of what might be the apparent repetition of some of the same principles and expectations. I've attempted to soften this repetition by couching it with slightly different perspectives or slices, supporting each in turn with varied Scriptures, writings, and personal experiences.

Related to this redundancy, perhaps you'll allow me a sports analogy taken from a book I enjoyed reading, *When Pride Still Mattered*, by the Pulitzer Prize-winning author David Maraniss. It's a biography of the legendary football coach, Vince Lombardi. Even today, many, if not most, regard him as the greatest football coach ever. This voluminous book notes some incredible detail about his life, which, yes, includes significant repetition. The author writes extensively of Lombardi's commitment to teaching and re-teaching the fundamentals of the game, such as blocking and tackling, as well as his continual repetition of the detailed components of every play in his classroom chalk talks. He kept fewer plays in his playbook than most teams in the National Football League (NFL). His routine was to go over each play in great detail, explaining the role of each player and why his specific responsibility was important to the success of the play. Lombardi demonstrated how the play would fail if someone missed his assignment. He did so for every position on the offense. He then did the same thing with his team out on the field. His men drilled every play incessantly. His goal was to have every single player know his responsibility on every play so well that he could go out on the field and perform his role without any hesitation because he knew exactly what was expected of him, as part of a team and as an individual.

Lombardi arrived in Green Bay, Wisconsin, in 1959 as the new head coach of the Green Bay Packers. Until his arrival, the Packers for many years had been considered the doormat of the National Football League after several seasons of losing records. Lombardi changed that reputation.

The Greatest Leap of Your Life

He began by winning the NFL Coach of the Year Award in 1959, and in 1960 he took the Packers to the championship game, where they lost to the Philadelphia Eagles.

Lombardi, while proud of his team, was not satisfied. His goal was for his Packers to become consistent champions. He wanted them to become the New York Yankees of football, and in the 1960s, they indeed did.

As he began training camp in 1961, he committed more strongly than ever to starting from scratch in the teaching of and re-teaching of plays and the fundamentals of football. He taught as though his players didn't know the game or couldn't remember a thing from the past two seasons. However, he probably got a bit carried away this particular year, as he opened the first session with his players by this most elemental statement: "Gentlemen," he said, holding the pigskin in his right hand, "this is a football," to which Max McGee (a veteran wide receiver and team comic) from the rear of the squad delivered the immortal Packer retort, "Uh, Coach, could you slow down a little. You're going too fast for us." McGee's line had even Lombardi chuckling, but not for long.

So it is with us Christians. We, too, need to discipline our time and our minds so that we spend time with God in prayer and the written Word to reinforce our understanding and faith in God's playbook for salvation, while giving thanks to Him each day for all of our blessings. This practice promotes the peace and joy that leads to further growth as a Christian.

Some of My Early Growth

As I mentioned earlier, I do not have a perfectly clear picture of how my initial growth in the Holy Spirit evolved and at what speed. I do know that daily prayer was a very powerful and meaningful exercise to strengthen my connection with God, Christ, and the Holy Spirit. As you proceed, I expect that you will see many things in a different light than before. As I began to grow through my teenage years, I developed a maturity about life that was enhanced through faith and prayer. I developed a deeper concern for my family and others on a consistent basis. I found a new excitement to life and living each day – one day at a time!

I recall a couple of modest examples of how I changed from the selfish kid described before my friend Joe's death into one who had gained peace and joy in his soul. Every winter after Joe Hosay died, I made sure that Mr. Hosay never shoveled another flake of snow. We got a lot of snow

The Greatest Leap of Your Life

in upstate New York, and that favor required a lot of shoveling. But I was determined to do his sidewalks and driveway first, before I did ours, just so that he never got the chance to get out there to do it himself. Clearing the walks and drive simply reflected the love in my heart for Joe and his family.

Still a bachelor at age twenty-four, I went into the Army following graduate school. I entered as a 2nd Lieutenant and came out as a Captain. I spent one of my three years in Vietnam. I provide this detail to let you know that I was in a position to save some money. While I certainly wasn't a hermit during those years, I was relatively frugal then because of a simple objective. I wanted to provide my parents and sister and brother-in-law with virtually all of my savings (I did keep $3,000 to buy a brand new white Volkswagen Kharmann Ghia convertible). I loved my family dearly, and I knew that this time was probably the only opportunity I would have to do such a thing, as I intended to have my own family someday. Further, I felt blessed and confident in my own economic future with an MBA in hand going into the exciting field of hospital administration. I relate these simple and modest examples not to boast; in fact, I'm a bit embarrassed to mention them, as they are not earth-shattering. But I think that this goal is a small demonstration of how a self-centered person like me can become totally different and more considerate of others – with God in his heart.

As I matured as a Christian, I wasn't concerned about what others thought about me. I just wanted to do things that reflected positively on God and Jesus, because I was so grateful to God for my love of life and the peace and joy that He had established in my life. I knew I didn't need to worry about many things that used to worry me as a kid. I was certain that God, through the Holy Spirit, would guide me in the right direction and that I need not fear anything. Jesus, in speaking to the disciple Thomas (remember "doubting Thomas"?) about the Holy Spirit said in John 14:26–28 NLT:

> But when the Father sends the Counselor as my representative—and by the Counselor I mean the Holy Spirit—he will teach you everything and will remind you of everything I myself have told you.
> I am leaving you with a gift—peace of mind and heart. And the peace I give isn't like the peace the world gives. So don't be troubled or afraid.

In a short anecdote, I'll relate a little sports tale here that relates to putting fear aside. While growing up, I had often gone to my future high school's football games. I loved watching the games, listening to that great U-E (Union-

The Greatest Leap of Your Life

Endicott) fight song, and dreaming about what a thrill it would be to play in front of two to five thousand people every Saturday in the fall. While I was reasonably athletic, through my sophomore year I had only focused on baseball and basketball. But in the summer before my junior year in high school, I got the itch to give football a try. I was lucky in that my backyard neighbor, Eileen Stancoti, was going out with the new season's co-captain, John DiOrio. Fortunately for me, Eileen and I were good friends, and at my behest, she asked John if he could get me into U-E's out-of-town, week-long, season-beginning training camp coming up at the end of August. I was fortunate that John liked Eileen a lot, as it still amazes me that John talked head coach Nick Di Nunzzio into letting a kid with no experience in organized football whatsoever into this intensive, opening of the season football camp. It probably didn't hurt that my JV baseball coach, George Cardone, was also an assistant football coach and may have vouched for me in some way as well.

    I went to camp full of optimism, intent on learning everything I could about offense and defense, and I went with absolutely no fear of anything. Boy, did I learn. We returned home and continued practices daily at the high school. I worked hard and was constantly running (half-back) plays

The Greatest Leap of Your Life

of Ithaca High School, U.E.'s opening season opponent, in practice.

Friday afternoon was the big day. The coaches began to call names, which obviously belonged to the varsity roster, the day before the opening game at Ithaca. I waited and waited, and then finally, after not hearing my name called, I heard, "Okay, the rest of you go back inside for a chalk talk." I was obviously a junior varsity player, not varsity. Once we returned to the classroom, I recall looking out the window at the varsity continuing their outdoor practice and feeling so envious.

At around 6:30 that evening, my parents pulled into the driveway from grocery shopping, and I went out to help bring in the bags. The phone rang, and either my mom or dad yelled that Keith Coleman was on the phone. Keith had called to tell me that I had been added to the roster for Saturday's game at Ithaca. He had packed my duffle bag, and I was to meet the team bus in the morning. Well, son of a gun if I didn't go and get inserted in the second half and do very well. I was so pumped when Coach put me in to return the second half kickoff. There were two of us back. When the ball was kicked, I hustled over to the other side of the field in front of the other back (who I'm sure was not happy) to

The Greatest Leap of Your Life

catch it, and I ran as hard as I could straight up the middle. That play was a very good runback that got me into several offensive plays in the second half. Beginning the following week, I was inserted in the starting lineup both offensively and defensively, where I remained for the rest of my junior and senior years. I was not an outstanding player, but my teammates and the coaching staff could count on me to do a good job game in and game out.

Believe it or not, playing high school football in front of all my friends and family and pretty big crowds was one of the great thrills of my youth. I know that working hard, having no fear, and possessing some athletic ability contributed to whatever success I had playing organized football. I have always thanked God for the opportunity to play this game in high school and my freshman year in college, after such a late exposure to organized football. Football offered more than just some great memories. It was an opportunity to learn and develop some very important attributes, such as teamwork and supporting people around you. I was so privileged later to watch my son for three years as his high school's starting quarterback, and I know he gained valuable life lessons from his experience as well. I brought this story into the book for two reasons. First, this opportunity was one of the small leaps in life when I know my faith put fear aside so that I was able to focus in a positive way on achieving success. Secondly, I learned a lesson in life from God as well. As we face opportunities, issues, or problems, if we stay focused on how we can succeed and the value of that success, rather than fearing the consequences of failure, we can be far more productive and optimistic in living our lives.

I have found sports to be one of the many exciting aspects to life. We all have so many blessings that we take for granted more than we should, including our work, our family, our leisure, our freedom, our health, and our abilities. We often need to remind ourselves of how blessed we are. I'll never forget the sense of thrill and gratitude I felt, out of the blue, one Saturday afternoon in 1999. While I was listening to the national anthem before one of my son's high school football games, I kept saying to myself: *You lucky stiff to be living in this wonderful free country and having the opportunity to watch your son play football on a Saturday afternoon.* I find that the closer I get to God and Christ, the more I appreciate my blessings.

Peace and Joy with Endurance

As we grow in the Holy Spirit, He will not only grant us strength and guidance for everyday living, but He will also open our eyes continually, not necessarily daily or weekly, to insights that bring either new or deeper meaning to life. This new relationship, as it matures, enables us to appreciate more fully the good things in our life that we often take for granted, such as our family, our work, our friends, and our freedom. This insight helps us better understand situations in our lives much more clearly than before. I have no doubt that, because of the Holy Spirit, born-again Christians are able to see many insightful things in life that others don't. Born-again Christians have this insight not because they are any better than their fellow human beings, but only because the Holy Spirit has taken up residence within them to guide their lives, and this communication and insight continue as long as they remain faithful and stay tuned. Interestingly, to the non-believer, this sort of statement can put up another barrier to taking the great leap, because it may sound foolish. Yet to the believer, this kind of reality only reinforces our faith.

The Greatest Leap of Your Life

God does not want His children to live unhappy, stressful, fearful lives. He loves us all dearly and equally, and He wants us all to have peace and joy in our lives. That desire doesn't mean that we won't have problems in life. We certainly will. But one of the great truths in God's Word that has been such a great source of strength and belief in my life is God's promise that He will never allow us to be given more than we can handle and that we need only trust and believe in Him for our strength and guidance throughout life. To gain perspective on this truth, I've turned to the following section, entitled "Where to Cast Your Care", in Billy Graham's book *Unto the Hills*:

> Has God left us alone to cope with the trials, tribulations, and temptations of life? I'm glad He has not! Jesus Christ, our Lord and Savior, has told us in specific terms just what we are to do about worry. The Bible offers a workable formula for care and anxiety.
>
> What are we to do about these past, present, and future worries? The Bible says that we are to cast them upon Him. Our guilty past, our anxious present, and the unknown future are all to be cast upon Christ. All of man's burdens and anxieties are wrapped up in these three words: past, present, and future. For the guilt of the past, God says: "I have redeemed thee" (Isaiah 44:2). "I have loved thee with an everlasting

love" (Jeremiah 31:3). "The blood of Jesus Christ his Son cleanseth us from all sin" (I John 1:7).

For the present Christ says: "I am with you always, even unto the end of the world" (Matthew 28:20). If the burden bearer is with us, then why should we be crushed by our burdens? The French translation of this phrase, "Cast all your care upon Him" is "Unload your distresses upon God." Have you ever seen a dump truck get rid of its load? It would be of no use if it carried its burden forever. The driver simply pushes a button or pulls on a lever and the heavy load is discharged at the prescribed spot.

We push the button of faith or pull the lever of trust, and our burden is discharged upon the shoulder of Him who said He would gladly bear it. Cast the anxious present upon Him, for He cares for you— says the Bible. The worries of the future are obliterated by His promises. "Take therefore no thought for the morrow. ... But seek ye first the kingdom of God, and his righteousness; and all these things shall be added unto you" (Matthew 6:34, 33). This promise, if we obey it, takes all the aimlessness out of life and puts purpose into it. It brings all life into balance, and earth's hours become so joyous that they blend into the glory of eternity. Boredom, fretfulness, and anxiety are lost in the wonder of His wonderful grace.

This trust is not escapism from the real world. While I believe in the promises above and the peace and joy their truth brings to me, I am a strong advocate of hard work and doing your best to control what you can control. Jesus said that you must count the costs when referring to the thinking and planning that goes into the realities of life, such as constructing a building or a home or developing a business. We have been given minds and the freedom of choice to exercise in building our lives and the lives of our families. We would be derelict if we didn't use these gifts in an optimal way.

However, we are finite and imperfect. We are not capable of solving alone everything that comes before us. That very limitation is why the above truth is so powerful for me. It gives me great peace and joy to know that I have a strength and support to lift me in good times and in bad times as well. We read in Philippians 4:6–7 RSV. "Have no anxiety about anything, but in everything by prayer and supplication with thanksgiving let your requests be made known to God. And the peace of God, which passes all understanding, will keep your hearts and your minds in Christ Jesus."

Life can be very difficult, and therefore peace and joy can sometimes appear to be elusive or far away. Jesus said: "These things I have spoken unto you, that in Me ye might have peace. In the world ye shall have tribulation, but be of good cheer; I have overcome the world" (John 16:33 KJV). Christ describes the peace and joy the great leap holds for us.

The Greatest Leap of Your Life

We all have to deal with different problems and issues on a daily basis. Some people seemingly have an easier or harder time than others. We really don't know how difficult or good life has been for others; we generally can only surmise from a distance and usually with little evidence what other people's lives are like. While my family has faced adversity like all other families, I can't imagine the anguish and level of difficulty that some have faced in losing children to disease, war, drugs, or accidental deaths. Certainly others have suffered equally devastating losses in one way or another. Because I have not had to face such devastating losses, I know that I have been more fortunate than others. The fact is that we all certainly face testing throughout life. A pastor named Reinhold Niebuhr (1892–1971) wrote a well-known prayer called the Serenity Prayer that has had a great impact on a large number of people. It reads:

> God, give us grace to accept with serenity
> the things that cannot be changed,
> Courage to change the things
> which should be changed,
> and the Wisdom to distinguish
> the one from the other.
>
> Living one day at a time,
> Enjoying one moment at a time,
> Accepting hardship as a pathway to peace,

The Greatest Leap of Your Life

Taking, as Jesus did,
This sinful world as it is,
Not as I would have it,
Trusting that You will make all things right,
If I surrender to Your will,
So that I may be reasonably happy in this life,
And supremely happy with You forever in the next.

Amen.

I have often felt that I am among the most blessed people in this world – overwhelmingly – because I know that Jesus Christ is my Lord and Savior and that I have life eternal ahead of me. I have these blessings not because of what I have done to deserve them, but because of what Jesus Christ did for me through His life, death, and resurrection. This fact has given me great peace and joy throughout my life. I, however, remain very imperfect in living as fully as Jesus has taught us. But I believe in Him, and I work to imitate Him daily. And that goal explains why I enjoy life so much. It's why I sleep well at night. It's the foundation of the optimism I bring to my personal and professional life. It's the reason I do not remain discouraged about anything for very long. I have felt the love, the peace, the joy, the insight, and the absolute strength of the Holy Spirit in my life virtually every day, gifts which provide me with a sense of calm and tranquility. Jesus said: "Peace I leave with you, my peace I give unto you: ... Let your heart not be troubled, neither let it be afraid" (John 14:27 KJV). This peace and joy is sometimes indescribable, but I can at least describe it as consistently soothing and comforting, enabling me to be a better person in life than I would otherwise be. I hope and pray that this peace and joy will become yours as you consider the greatest leap of your life.

Chapter VIII

Our Responsibility—Keep the Leap Flowing

Why This Book

As we reach the final two chapters, I thought I should comment on why this book was important for me to write.

When I left the hospital field, I took an opportunity to begin a less time consuming occupation in the field of executive and professional benefits, as well as some promotional work for a couple of quality organizations. Obviously this job is less stressful than running a hospital, with its consistently twelve-hour days within a very complex organization and its multitude of constituencies. I refer to this new stage of life as Chapter II. My priority for the rest of my life is to balance my new work with the following priorities:

First, I wish to grow spiritually daily so that I can become a better person and servant for my Lord's kingdom.

Secondly, I will keep busy with work and eventually find the optimal form of volunteerism so that I can give back to others the blessings I have received in my own life.

Third, I want to write a book for my family, so that they can more fully understand my faith. Among my daily prayers is that my entire family will find and accept Jesus as their Lord and Savior. That one priority has a very special emotional attachment for me.

Fourthly, I now have the desire to see if this book can get published, in some fashion, so that it might reach others who might find it helpful in finding God's peace and His plan for salvation. I have never been one to wear my faith on my sleeve, as noted in the Preface. While my family knows of my strong faith, I have perhaps failed miserably in my responsibility here in not proclaiming Christ in front of others. While I have done so in a number of discussions with family and friends, I certainly haven't engaged in any consistent, in-depth, or widespread effort. Right or wrong, I have never wanted to conduct myself aggressively concerning my beliefs in a way that would discourage people from seeking God or Christ. I chose not to bring my faith into professional or social settings as a general rule.

On the one hand, I could make a case that this decision demonstrates a weakness in my faith. I can only say that I have always had a strong desire not to cause anyone to dislike the truth about Christ. I have observed that Christianity, when brought up in certain settings or consistently brought up in virtually any setting, can and does run the risk of compromising a Christian's effectiveness in eventually having a positive impact for Christianity on others. I have chosen not to smother others with what I believe, but I will enthusiastically talk of my beliefs when the occasion arises for such discussion. Therefore, I could say that I have taken the easy road and have been derelict in my responsibilities to Christ.

As a means of perhaps trying to compensate for my lack of witness for Him, I am going to try to publish this book in an effort to reach more than my family. I believe I have an important message to impart that I've tried to express simply with at least some depth and what I consider important repetition. I hope that this work might touch lives for Christ when people read it for the first time or refer to it at a later time as part of my effort to "keep the leap flowing."

Fulfillment and Responsibility

If or when you take the leap and accept the astonishing fact that God did indeed come down to earth in the form of the divine-man as His Son, Jesus Christ, to die for your sins so that you can be born again, then you accept the responsibility to live your life as Jesus has taught us to live it. Keeping your great leap of faith flowing in your life then becomes your responsibility.

For all Christians, this duty is simultaneously an awesome responsibility, a challenging task, and if fulfilled, the most rewarding and gratifying experience of our lives. Jesus came to earth to teach us how best to live and to meet the standards of our Father in heaven. He died on the cross for our sins as the necessary reconciliation of God's hatred of our sins with His great love for us. Jesus rose from the dead to demonstrate the reality of the life after death made possible in Christ's sacrifice and resurrection for all those who accept Christ as their Savior and Lord and genuinely repent of their sins. In this rebirth, we now have the wonderful yet difficult challenge of living consistently with the standards Jesus espoused and embodied while here on earth. Who better to show us and teach us how to live our lives than God, who created us in His own image, understands our basic needs, and loves us so dearly?

You will likely ask, "How can I live this way? The bar is set so high." I concede that the challenge is not only great but is simply impossible if we think we can meet it alone. We are not capable of living as God expects without the strength of God and Christ through the Holy Spirit. Even then, because we are human and imperfect, we will experience breakdowns and failures along the way. But if we remain faithful, we can move away from inclination to regular sin in our lives towards sin as the exception rather than the rule, and in the process we can find a peace and joy that is beyond expectation or explanation. What sets the Holy Spirit apart for me from anything else in life is the incredible touch of reinforcement that comes from Him that strengthens, calms, and encourages me with a peace that is so special that I know it can only come from an infinite God of love. As such times, I remember that finite man has been given something very special as a foundation for his life that can help him both to withstand the temptations and to face the other challenges in this world.

When we are genuinely born again, we take on a new self, just as if we have shed the old self and have donned something new with a built-in power to live a different life based on different priorities and beliefs that will begin to have an impact on our outlook in life. This new exhilaration and excitement at being alive comes from a new sense of peace, purpose, and optimism. This new sense of life may have variations, as we are all different individuals in one way or another. The extent and timing of this new self-evolving change will vary among all born-again Christians.

Four Constants to Remember in Our Growth

As you take on this new life, whether you're in the early days and months or in your second, tenth, twentieth, or fiftieth year since being born again, remembering the following four constants is very important. First, God loves us all and truly wants us to learn to live our lives more abundantly here on earth, and He has given us the road map to do so. Secondly, He knows that we will falter from time to time, but He is always there to forgive us and strengthen us. We need only sincerely ask for both. The third constant is that, no matter how difficult life might get, He will never give us more than we can handle if we remain faithful to Him and to our Lord and Savior Jesus Christ.

Fourthly, remember that following His resurrection, Jesus said that He must leave to join His Father in heaven so that He might provide the Comforter (the Holy Spirit) to those who believe. When we are born again, the Holy Spirit truly begins to reside in our souls and becomes our constant guide, strength, and insight into leading our new lives with our newly emerging self. Remember, the Holy Spirit is God, and He establishes a permanent residence within you. In and through this connection, we receive a basis or foundation of power and direction that is exciting, challenging, and peaceful.

Though this chapter is important for me to write, frankly, it may be the most difficult to write, because I feel the need to balance the importance of striving to reach the very high bar of responsible, holy living established throughout the New Testament, including the teachings and life of Christ, and the stark reality that we are not capable of that perfection day in and day out. Far from it. Thus, we will fail or breach our duties along the way, as has been my imperfect experience as well.

We have been exposed to something new and extraordinary, and the bar of acceptability, of what is good and not good, has been raised considerably. I feel that we absolutely must understand that we should not be discouraged when we do sin and do things that our new self, with the Holy Spirit as our conscience, knows are wrong. Instead, this new life calls for us to get back to our feet, reaching out to God for forgiveness and the strength to do better. He is with us, and He will stay close. But we must also have the resiliency in our faith to rebound and ask for His help to remain committed and strong. And this resiliency is all very doable because the Holy Spirit is within us to guide and strengthen us. The Christian life definitely gets better and easier as we mature and remain disciplined in this process of growth, but because we are imperfect, it's never perfect.

The Challenge to Commit

We live in an incredibly complex world filled with much information, many activities and responsibilities, a slew of distractions and temptations, and a pace of life that is sometimes overwhelming. As a result, we often don't seem to be able to find enough quality and quantitative time with our children, spouses, parents, relatives, neighbors, co-workers, and strangers to learn more about them and their needs and what we might do to help and support them. We are too often interrupted with the phone to answer, the favorite sports event to watch (certainly one of my many weaknesses), the bills to pay, the house to clean, the lawn to mow, the garden to plant and weed, the kids' school and sports activities to follow, the homework to supervise, or our own work to finish. Then, of course, we would all like to have a little time to ourselves for that favorite hobby, such as golf, fishing, reading, jogging, lifting, listening to the classics or opera, or mixing that cocktail before dinner.

You will learn that among the very important responsibilities of the born-again Christian is commitment. This commitment includes praying and reading the Bible and other insightful readings by Christian authors daily. I simply can't overemphasize the importance of dedication to these practices on a daily basis which has, as stated before, an analogy to the professional athlete.

In order for athletes to fulfill their responsibilities to themselves, their teams, and their fans, they must exercise their bodies and hone their skills on a consistent, daily basis. On a more common note, for those of us who want to lose weight or at least stay even, we, too, must be consistent with our workouts and diets. If we are inconsistent in our dedication to either, we can get off track and become ineffective in our quest to keep in shape and remain healthy. We must have the same vigilance as born-again Christians with prayer and Bible reading on a regular basis, or we will lose our edge and our ability to maximize our effectiveness in living our lives to the standard that Christ has set for us. Despite the distractions and responsibilities noted earlier, it's very important we carve out a quality period of time or times during the course of the day to reinforce and enhance our knowledge, understanding, and faith in what we have accepted in this new relationship with God and our Savior.

Why This Commitment Is So Important

In terms of developing and maintaining a healthy body, we must discipline ourselves to have the staying power to exercise consistently and daily and with the same degree of effort, even on the days when doing so seems extraordinarily difficult. This type of dedication now exists for the born-again Christian in terms of learning from the Bible and learning how to pray and have fellowship with God on a daily basis. This consistency reminds us daily of God's love for us. It helps us remember the sacrifices and teachings of our Savior and the responsibilities we have now shouldered to live a better life of faith, trust, and surrender to Him because of all He has sacrificed for us through His love. Christ's teachings were incredibly insightful and full of wisdom about life, eternity, and the importance of prayer. Regular focus on this routine enables us to mature, allowing us to extend hope to our families and neighbors in a more helpful and supportive way. As we grow as Christians, through the Holy Spirit, we become more insightful and find life more exciting and peaceful than ever before.

Should we get lazy in this commitment, we clearly run the risk of not staying connected to God, Christ, and the Holy Spirit. As we slack off, the relationship can become more distant and begin to affect the way we live our lives. We more easily fall back to doing things and thinking things that were our way of life prior to being born again, things which can include living in the practice of sin rather than committing sin as the exception.

You may say: "Life is already too crammed with pressures. How can I fit in any more?" That logical question is one that all born-again Christians must ask.

Those who find this discipline too difficult to include and never accept it as a daily exercise are very likely to become stagnant or perhaps depleted Christians. Though they may have been blessed to come to understand the Great News of Christ, they have lost the lasting truth in their hearts and souls to overwhelming counter forces, and they have found it difficult to dedicate themselves to the practices necessary to keep this great blessing in their hearts and minds on a daily basis for the rest of their earthly lives.

Grasping and Retaining

Jesus beautifully and concisely described this acceptance and retention of things that are important in life in one of His parables in Mark 4 1:20 NLT:

> Once again Jesus began teaching by the lakeshore. There was such a large crowd along the shore that he got into a boat and sat down and spoke from there. He began to teach the people by telling many stories such as this one:
> "Listen! A farmer went out to plant some seed. As he scattered it across his field, some seed fell on a footpath, and the birds came and ate it. Other seed fell on shallow soil with underlying rock. The plant sprang up quickly, but it soon wilted beneath the hot sun and died because the roots had no nourishment in the shallow soil. Other seed fell among the thorns that shot up and choked out the tender blades so that it produced no grain. Still other seed fell on fertile soil and produced a crop that was thirty, sixty, and even a hundred times as much as had been planted."

Then he said, "Anyone who is willing to hear should listen and understand!"

Later, when Jesus was alone with the twelve disciples and with the others who were gathered around, they asked him, "What do your stories mean?"

He replied, "You are permitted to understand the secret about the Kingdom of God. But I am using these stories to conceal everything about it from outsiders, so that the Scriptures might be fulfilled:

"They see what I do, but they don't perceive its meaning.

They hear my words, but they don't understand.

So they will not turn from their sins and be forgiven."

"But if you can't understand this story, how will you understand all the others I am going to tell? The farmer I talked about is the one who brings God's message to others. The seed that fell on the hard path represents those who hear the message, but then Satan comes at once and takes it away from them. The rocky soil represents those who hear the message and receive it with joy. But like young plants in such soil, their roots don't go very deep. At first they get along fine, but they wilt as soon as they have problems or are persecuted because they believe the word. The thorny ground represents those who hear and accept the Good News, but all too quickly the message is crowded out by the cares of this life, the lure of wealth, and the desire for nice things, so no crop is produced. But the good soil represents those who hear and accept God's message and produce a huge harvest—thirty, sixty, or even a hundred times as much as had been planted."

I believe this parable speaks, in part, to our need to exercise our spiritual minds through the Bible, prayer, and meditation on spiritual things in order to retain its freshness and drive its roots deep. One thing that never ceases to amaze me is that the exercise I mentioned brings forth through the guidance of the Holy Spirit new knowledge, reinforcement of the old, and insight that strengthens our relationship with God. It provides a better understanding of what He expects of us, presents a clearer perception of life, generates a capacity for tolerating others, and enhances a closeness to Him so that, when we periodically falter (or should I say even daily falter), the closeness to Him and His love enables us to bounce back on track more easily, seeking forgiveness and guidance to do better.

There Will Be Stumbles – A Few of Mine

I wish to acknowledge here that, while I was born again over fifty years ago and have lived a life with values learned through Christ that have never left my being, during some significant periods I did not exercise daily or regularly in prayer, reading of the Bible, and other important writings, and I periodically lost my intimate connection with God.

The Greatest Leap of Your Life

For example, through college, military service, and prior to my marriage in 1973, I regularly partook in the joy of female relationships that was such a big part of my life and the lives of my friends and acquaintances during this period. Certainly as I got further away from my spiritual exercise, my spiritual mind and soul lost their edge. They became more filled with lusts and harmful thought processes that were previously not prevalent when I was closer to God and Christ. During those periods, I lost some of the positive virtues of tolerance and patience with others and the compassion and respect for others to the extent and level that I previously had. My lusts and impatience impacted my principles and respect for others. Certainly other deficiencies appeared as well. Comparatively speaking, from the world's view I was probably still considered a reasonably decent person, but from God's perspective I know that was not true. But because of His incredible love, He did not abandon me, though I deserved His absence.

During these times, a couple of fears that were inconsistent with my faith and even with my previous comfort level developed in my life. Initially, I loved public speaking and was quite good at it. I recall when I was a young administrative resident at Fairfax Hospital in Falls Church, Virginia,

The Greatest Leap of Your Life

that Steve Lannon, vice president for planning and facilities, was making numerous presentations on the hospital's new building project, taking the hospital from three hundred twenty-five to six hundred sixty beds. (Fairfax Hospital went on to become one of the finest hospitals and hospital systems in the country.) I asked if I could participate with him. He agreed, and once I began, Steve started giving me the bulk of the presentations. We were presenting to audiences of between fifty and four hundred people at a time. Presenting the information was great fun for me. I know that Steve saw it was natural for me, and he liked the job I was doing. I made a number of presentations in the military and certainly at my first job out of the military at Memorial Hospital in Worcester, Massachusetts.

I arrived at Memorial Hospital in 1971 after I received my MBA from George Washington University in 1968 and spent three years in the service. I couldn't wait to absorb everything. I wanted to get my organizational line responsibilities as soon as possible, and I was spending a great deal of time, including weekends, at the hospital. I was perhaps working too much while burning the candle at both ends, spending the nights out during the week and weekends typical of a lot of bachelors.

The Greatest Leap of Your Life

One day while I was in the cafeteria, something happened that frightened me. I felt like something in my mind clicked off and then back on. The sensation was very disturbing to me. Even today, I can't explain or describe the experience very well. I felt as though my confidence had been shaken from this episode, and one of the strange, residual effects of this experience was that I developed a fear of public speaking. How that fear occurred is difficult to comprehend, but it was a fact. That new fear was a bit traumatic for a guy who needed to speak publicly in his current position and certainly needed to do so a great deal later on, if my eventual intent was to become the CEO of a hospital. The fear was such a problem that I could be miserable for days prior to any significant presentation. This change took place after several years of losing my discipline to God, prayer, and reading the Bible. These mid-college years (mid 1960s) to then, when I was sowing oats like a lot of young men my age, I got away from the connection with God, Jesus, and the Holy Spirit that had molded me in the values I had accepted for my life.

Despite this periodic uneasiness with public speaking, God has helped me through this responsibility for four decades. Only my wife Judy has known of my fear. However, she tells me after I speak that she does not see any discomfort at all. Well, speaking to a crowd is still not a piece of cake. I am, however, determined to reach that same comfort level of public speaking that was once a joy and a very natural activity for me.

I also developed another phobia – flying. I initially enjoyed flying, but then I developed a dislike and fear of flying. The fear was not of crashing; essentially, the claustrophobic sense of being up in the air and not being able to get out has been the culprit for me. For most of my twenties, I loved flying, and I had been a constant flier in the States as well as overseas in the Army, from 1968–71. This time span involved my tour in Vietnam, which included many helicopter flights north, south, and west from where I was stationed in Quin Nohn. R & R trips during that time took me to Sydney, Australia, and Bangkok, Thailand, as well as many stand-by military flights in the States. But for much of my life, though my family and I have certainly flown across country to several destinations on family vacation trips, I've not been ecstatic about flying. I inappropriately used 9/11 as a solid excuse to stay away from flying as well. I am now determined to deal with this issue, because the inconsistency bothers me. I truly have such strong faith in God and Christ,

The Greatest Leap of Your Life

yet I've unwittingly, but selfishly, denied my wife some wonderful opportunities for travel because I wouldn't deal with my discomfort.

One of a number of examples of this selfishness relates to an opportunity to vacation at a gorgeous villa in Spain overlooking the ocean. In my position as a hospital CEO, I became acquainted with a fascinating man, Covington Hardee. A Harvard Law School professor and graduate, "Cuz" went on to become CEO of a New York City bank. Following his retirement, we recruited him to become volunteer chairman of a major hospital capital campaign. This recruitment was the beginning of a very long and strong friendship. Numerous times he asked me to use his villa in Spain for family vacations, and I selfishly turned him down because of this fear of flying. My wife, though very disappointed, is an incredibly understanding woman. But this missed opportunity serves as an example of how in some areas I reverted to a way of doing things that I realize I need, want, and intend to change.

Don't Ever Be Discouraged For Long

I will fight sin and weakness, as we all will, every day of my life. The temptations of life, such as lust, materialism, selfishness, power-seeking, jealousy, coveting, and the like, will always haunt mankind. And I have had failures along the way, for certain, and just as certainly, I will remain imperfect. I can say that, because of the Holy Spirit's influence on my life, my standards for defining sin are higher than the standards of perhaps others who are not so influenced. While that difference may be true, it's irrelevant. God expects that, to whom much is given, much is expected. I know better; therefore, my standard should be higher.

More importantly, I think it is critical never to give up on God because of your guilt for past sins committed. He will never give up on you during your life. Never give up on yourself to live a better, more productive, happy life. He only asks that you come to Him in faith, repenting of your sins, and accept Jesus Christ as your Lord and Savior, trusting Him to guide, protect, and love you. While we can find comfort in knowing that God will not give up on us, we will all come to a time when it will be too late, and none of us can know in advance when that time might arrive.

Continuing Our Growth or Flow

As we come closer to Him, our recognition of what is sinful is much more sensitive, and therefore we will perceive that we are simply not capable of living a perfectly sinless life. But through the guidance and strength of the Holy Spirit, we can make sin, as I said earlier, more the exception than the rule in our lives. Through the Holy Spirit, we also gain enormous insight into life that gives us the wisdom and capacity that drives us to be better people, more helpful, more respectful, and more loving of our family and our neighbors. While some might think of this insight as a huge restriction on their lives, learning new things about life, God, ourselves, and those around us is actually more liberating.

Christ gave us so much wisdom through the example He set for us and through His teachings. He delivered one such powerful statement when the Pharisees confronted Him:

> But when the Pharisees heard that he had silenced the Sadducees with his reply, they thought up a fresh question of their own to ask him. One of them, an expert in religious law, tried to trap him with this question: "Teacher, which is the most important commandment in the law of Moses?"
> Jesus replied, "'You must love the Lord your God with all your heart, all your soul, and all your

mind.' This is the first and greatest commandment. A second is equally important: 'Love your neighbor as yourself.'" All the other commandments and all the demands of the prophets are based on these two commandments."

Matthew 22:34–40 NLT

As I strive to reach living this greatest of all commandments and the other teachings of Jesus, I have found that I am blessed with an even greater capacity to love each member of my family. When you think about how much you love your family anyway, just think about the capacity to love and appreciate them even more! I also find that this capacity has impacted positively my tolerance, understanding, and love for others. This sort of reinforcement merely enhances the continual flow from the greatest leap of your life.

Some Examples of Such Growth

One of the strengths I brought to my occupation as a hospital CEO was my relationship building within and outside of the organization. I like and respect people of all walks of life. This quality has been deeply driven into my soul because I believe that God created each one of us and that He loves each and every one of us equally. Knowing that truth, I can easily show respect for every human being I know.

Respect for People

A couple of examples might be appropriate here. First, I'll comment on our hospital's acceptance into the prestigious New York Presbyterian Health Care System. In the early to mid-1990s, there was a great frenzy for hospitals to affiliate in some fashion or merge with other hospitals. We completed a very extensive study of this trend that included four or five solid options. We decided that our top priority was to affiliate (not merge) with the Columbian Presbyterian Health Care System based in New York City. Their focus was to partner with quality hospitals that were also doing well financially and delivering excellent patient care within the tri-state area (New York, New Jersey, Connecticut). They were not interested in taking over hospitals via merger or other control mechanisms, but instead wanted to form a nucleus of quality hospitals that could work together on clinical programs and joint ventures that would increase both quality of care and volume of patients involved within the network. This affiliation was, in some ways, the opposite approach to system development of one of their chief competitors, New York Cornell Hospital, in mid-Manhattan.

In preparation for the key meeting that followed earlier preliminary meetings and exchanges of data, I assembled a small group to meet with the number two executive at Columbia Presbyterian, Mark Lory, who clearly was the number one decision maker on acceptance into the network. As part of this group, I included one of our very talented physicians (Harvard, Yale, and Columbia credentials) who, while difficult at times, was a charmer that could talk a dog off a meat wagon if necessary. While he and I had a contentious, roller coaster relationship, I respected him as a human being and admired the traits I knew he could bring to the table that day to help us bring the affiliation home for our hospital and our community. The other representatives in this group were also the right people to help us hit the home run we needed at this session.

The meeting was scheduled for 4:00, and everybody was on time except Mark Lory. As 4:30 came and then 4:45, I did my best to keep anyone from leaving. Mark called around 4:50 and apologized that his driver got lost. Though they thought they were only going to be a half hour late, now they were clearly still thirty to forty minutes away, and Mark wanted to know if we wanted to reschedule. The answer was an emphatic no. I was able to convince my entire group to stay, and we eventually had an excellent meeting in which everyone's questions were answered. Apparently from comments and body language, we reached a mutual decision that New Milford Hospital was about to become the first Connecticut affiliate of the Columbia Presbyterian Health Care System. The previously described doctor was terrific and instrumental to this very successful meeting. Had I not respected him as a human being, despite our periodic intense conflicts, I might have burned a bridge that could have precluded him from being a positive participant in this very important meeting. The New York Presbyterian System was formed in 1999, when Columbia Presbyterian Medical Center and New York Cornell Medical Center merged, and the new system included a combined total of over thirty hospitals in the tri-state system. This organization has become one of the most successful systems in the country. The point here is that we should strive for tolerance and respect for our fellow beings as a matter of principle, but unanticipated benefits can also result from such efforts.

Creating Success with Compassion

The other example I would relate is not unique to me, as I know that most of my colleagues view their employees as family as well. However, I can tell you that what drove me to work so hard, and hopefully smart, was the personal responsibility I felt to everyone who worked at that hospital to make the right decisions that would enable the hospital to be successful, thus securing our employees' jobs while doing what was best for our patients. Making those decisions entailed monitoring expenses, creating a work atmosphere that fostered employee loyalty to the hospital and its patients, and growing the volume of patient revenues by adopting quality programs that would draw and meet patients' needs, including an effective and ongoing physician recruitment program. While one of our annual objectives was to achieve a positive bottom line, two considerations tempered that goal. We first looked at putting appropriate new resources in to our staffing patterns in order to enhance patient care and employee satisfaction. Secondly, we gave back to our employees twenty to twenty-five percent of our fiscal year-end operating bottom line (excess revenue over expenses) in the form of bonuses just before Christmas. This gift was particularly important to the lower-paid employees who were such a vital part of our team effort.

Developing such an atmosphere benefitted the comfort and care given to our patients. And these improvements did not happen overnight or easily. They required hard work by a great team of people. I believe that we did so well for so long because the core of what drove us was our respect for one another and our work ethic that was determined to achieve our goals. In nearly thirty years, we had an enviable record of positive bottom lines, growth of quality programs, and strong growth in employment that did, unfortunately, include two minor layoffs. One was in the early nineties, and the other was in 2006. Prior to 2006, we completed fourteen of the previous fifteen years with a positive bottom line from operations.

Following our first loss from operations in seven years, in FY (fiscal year) 2006, we developed a FY 2007 budget that put the hospital back in the black by $600,000 after just four months into the new FY, when I left at the end of January 2007. The hospital finished that fiscal year with a $400,000 surplus. I'm pleased to say that the hospital was poised for another long run of meeting future challenges while maintaining job security with the continuation of good management and physician recruitment. Knowing what the administrative team had accomplished for our employees, patients, and community for so long was very important to me as I departed in 2007.

Respect and compassion for others are just two of many by-products that can result from a genuine and consistent relationship with God. It can also bring greater patience in your life and greater tolerance of people, their ideas, and their relationships. However, I don't mean to say that we can achieve Utopia. I certainly have had issues with people and personalities from time to time in my life and hospital responsibilities. But by and large, relationship building is the key to success in running a hospital or any other organization, and I believe that New Milford Hospital built such relationships pretty well for a long period of time. Whatever I contributed to that success owed its foundation, in part, to the principles of my faith.

Taking a Stand – The Dichotomy Concerning Tolerance

Though this brief section may appear to be a diversion, I hope that my readers stay with me, as I feel that the following topic is important for me to include.

A real dichotomy exists for me concerning the tolerance I mention as being a very important part of Christianity. And the root of that dichotomy is the belief that the narrow road to life eternal in heaven with our Creator leads only through belief and acceptance of Jesus Christ as our Savior through His death on the cross to atone for our sins.

The Old Testament clearly predicts the coming of the Messiah numerous times. The New Testament, of course, focuses on the Messiah. In Matthew 7:13-14 KJV, Jesus says, "Enter ye at the strait gate ... because strait is the gate, and narrow is the way; which leadeth unto life." Christ further said in Matthew 12:30 KJV, "He that is not with me is against me." In John 3:36 KJV, Jesus said: "He that believeth on the Son hath everlasting life: and he that believeth not the Son shall not see life; but the wrath of God abideth on him."

I know that this doctrine rings of the "holy roller" mentality of intolerance toward other beliefs. Also, it appears to contradict the great tolerance inherent in Christianity and the teachings of Jesus, i.e.: "love your enemies ... turn the other cheek ... do not judge others ... get the board out of your own eyes before you attempt to remove the slivers from others." I accept the wisdom of these teachings of Christ, and I believe that they are very important in our relationships with others.

But is this particular narrow element of Christianity that hard to accept? Look at the intolerance we have in our man-made laws; we will not accept murder, kidnapping, robbery, rape, or assault without punishment. Society must levy a consequence that reflects our intolerance of such acts. Why should an infinite God be any less tolerant of us? I believe that He came down to earth in the form of His Son Jesus Christ to teach us how to live our lives and to set the standard through example. He left us with a wealth of teachings recorded in the Bible and went through a painstaking torture and death to atone for all the sins of God's children. He rose from the dead to defeat the power and the fear of death with a promise of life eternal in heaven with Him and our Father. He sent the Holy Spirit to guide and strengthen us throughout our lives. Why would God, whose knowledge and love is infinite, go to such unfathomable lengths to develop an ultimate plan of salvation, describe it for the entire world to see and know, and not expect His plan to be the one and only road to salvation? God does not allow for multiple choice here. God is a Spirit who is infinite and who remains unchanged in what He expects of His children. God never changes. Through the prophets and others, He has left us with His expectations as recorded in the Bible. He has left no room for error or interpretation on this matter. I believe that Christ is the Messiah, the only way to salvation and eternal happiness with God our Father.

I know how this position can generate hostility in many people's minds about me and Christianity. But potential hostility should not compromise the truth about what you believe. I'm only hoping that through the Holy Spirit this book can touch lives for Christ and God's plan for our salvation.

God has lovingly given us a free will to do as we please and to believe as we please. We Americans live in a wonderful country that espouses freedom of religion. I support everyone's right to worship and to believe as he wishes, and I believe that virtually all Americans of all faiths subscribe to the same ideal. Someone might ask, "Isn't it hypocritical to espouse tolerance while you state that the only way to salvation and life eternal is through Christ?" In response, I would offer the following. I believe that God's enormous measure of love, mercy, and forgiveness provides incredible tolerance for our shortcomings. Therefore, how could I, with all of my transgressions, not try my best to be tolerant and patient with my fellow human beings as we all struggle to live our lives as best we can? I do my best, imperfectly, to live in tolerance. I realize that my belief that eternal life with God is only possible through Christ lays such tolerance open to criticism.

I have many friends, colleagues, co-workers, and relatives of all faiths that I love and with whom I enjoy spending time and working and sharing. I support with all my being everyone's right to his beliefs and opinions. But my love doesn't change the fact that God hates sin and a sinful life so deeply that He chose to come down to earth in the form of His Son Jesus Christ to die as a substitute for our sin, which He detests. Only such a sacrifice to reconcile the sin of the world would suffice for Him to forgive our sin and enable His children (all of us throughout the world, past, present, and future) to have eternal life with Him. Therefore, I believe in the one and only Messiah predicted and described throughout the Old Testament of the Bible. I believe that the one God who exists and created this earth and each one of us developed one plan of redemption and salvation.

I do not intend to be self-righteous. I know that I am human, imperfect, and certainly limited with what I absolutely know and can prove. I'm fallible like everyone else.

And everyone else has the right to independent beliefs. We are what we believe, and what I described above is what I deeply believe. If this belief labels me as intolerant, then I accept that judgment, and I do so in confidence and faith.

Flowing, Stagnant, or Depleted

We all have responsibilities within our families, our work, and our communities, whether we are parents, spouses, siblings, friends, co-workers, fellow countrymen, or fellow human beings. We all need to work at those responsibilities if we are to care for people and fulfill their needs. The doctor needs to stay current with his knowledge about the ever-changing findings in medicine and research. The lawyer must remain well-versed and conversant with the laws affecting his clients' needs. The mechanic must learn about all the electronic changes to the vehicles he is responsible for maintaining and repairing. The executive must stay attuned to the external trends and competition and facilitate and encourage teamwork in an organization, in order to lead it in a proper direction for success. Creators of the arts must learn about their crafts and hone their skills. The customer relations representative must constantly exercise skills that include listening with compassion and working efficiently in order to serve the customer optimally as well as the company that employs him. The carpenter, painter, and roofer must stay abreast of new and more effective products and ways of delivering their services so that their customers receive a better final product.

Among the major responsibilities of a Christian is first to recognize the responsibility of what you have just accepted in your life.

The Cost to Maintaining Your Leap

There is a cost to following Christ. There is an effort involved in staying strong in order to become and remain an effective follower. There is a flowing that is necessary for the Christian to be an effective instrument for Christ and His Kingdom and to maintain the flavor of his salt. There is a commitment necessary to maintain vitality in one's faith, trust, and surrender to something far bigger and far more important than one's self or anything else on this earth.

Three things are extremely important to remember that can make the difference between flowing rather than becoming stagnant or depleted. First, we must completely surrender to Christ through the Holy Spirit and constantly be filled with the Holy Spirit. Secondly, we must maintain a complete trust and faith in Him. Thirdly, we must daily sharpen our capacity to do so through praying and reading the Bible and other books and writings that interpret and provide insight into the teachings of the Bible and Christ. Commitment to these three actions on a daily basis will keep the flowing of the Holy Spirit's influence in our hearts and minds that provides a consistent and vibrant freshness to our faith.

Ephesians 5:18 NLT says "Let the Holy Spirit fill and control you." Jesus promised that the Holy Spirit would guide, protect, and strengthen us in good times and bad. So He said:

> "Take no thought, saying, What shall we eat? or, What shall we drink? or, Wherewithal shall we be clothed? ... But seek ye first the kingdom of God ... and all these things shall be added unto you" (Matthew 6:31, 33 KJV).

> "Ask, and it shall be given you; seek, and ye shall find; knock, and it shall be opened unto you" (Matthew 7:7 KJV).

Too often we are overcome with the pressures and distractions of this world, and at times we can become despondent. One story that speaks to this weakness involves one of our great Christian leaders taken from *Unto the Hills*, pages 316–317:

> There is a story about Martin Luther going through a period of depression and discouragement. For days his long face graced the family table and dampened the family's home life. One day his wife came to the breakfast table all dressed in black, as if she were going to a funeral service. When Martin asked her who had died, she replied, "Martin, the way you've been behaving lately, I thought God had died, so I came prepared to attend His funeral."
>
> Her gentle but effective rebuke drove straight to Luther's heart, and as a result of that lesson the great Reformer resolved never again to allow worldly care, resentment, depression, discouragement, or frustration to defeat him. By God's grace, he vowed, he would submit his life to the Savior and reflect His grace in a spirit of rejoicing, whatever came.

If despondency can afflict Martin Luther, it certainly can afflict us. We must be resilient in our faith.

The Greatest Leap of Your Life

Standing Out – Natural and Genuine

We Christians should naturally and genuinely stand out among the crowd with our friendliness, peaceful demeanor, cheerful and upbeat attitude, interest in others, approachability, and optimism, which reflect the great security, joy, and peace that we genuinely have through God's love and Christ's sacrifice. And this difference will come naturally as we mature and grow in our faith, commitment, and thanksgiving for what we have received.

Let me relate a good example of this truth, Dr. Norman Vincent Peale. In the mid-1980s, we restructured the hospital to create a holding company that included four subsidiaries. The hospital itself became a subsidiary, and we also created a fundraising foundation as one of the four subsidiaries. The prime objective of the foundation was to raise money for the hospital. One of our first tasks was to recruit board members that could help with that objective. I was most fond of two such members recruited: Janet Fisher and Dr. Norman Vincent Peale.

Janet was a very bright and classy lady who loved the hospital and was very involved with her husband Avery Fisher (of Avery Fisher Hall at Lincoln Center in New York City) in their own significant foundation in New York City. (Avery, a fascinating man, explained to me one day how he started his mega-million dollar Fisher Electronics out of his garage while he was working for an insurance company.) Despite Janet's work with their foundation, she also staunchly supported our hospital, which she promoted among her friends. She and Avery had a second home in the town of Washington, Connecticut, which was part of the hospital's service area. She had great pizzazz, class, and presence and was widely respected. She knew how to call a spade a spade and always offered sage advice. I enjoyed our friendship immensely. And following a surgical admission to our hospital, Avery became a big booster of the hospital as well. This husband and wife were wonderful people and ardent philanthropists.

Dr. Peale was the very well-known pastor of the Marble Collegiate Church in New York City and an author of several books, including the major best-seller in the 1950s or 60s, *The Power of Positive Thinking*. He and his wife Ruth also founded the Foundation for Christian Living in Pawling, New York, which is about twenty-five minutes from New Milford Hospital. Dr. Peale was generous to our foundation, and an effective advocate for the hospital. He was a gem of a man who became a good friend to me. We corresponded and met on a regular basis, though I didn't discuss my faith with him, or he with me.

This man of God walked the walk of optimism and faith. I probably spent a total of thirty to forty hours over a number of years with him, and I can tell you that he flowed with enthusiasm for life through his speech, mannerisms, and the bounce in his step. But what stood out for me most were his eyes. His eyes twinkled like I've never seen before or since, speaking volumes about how this man was filled with joy, faith, and optimism. He clearly lived what he preached. This kind of presence is what is meant by the statement that we Christians should naturally and genuinely stand out among the crowd because of our relationship with our God and our Savior. I will always remember and be grateful to him for going out of his way to meet my parents and sign one of his books for them. They were thrilled.

The Higher Standard and Ever-Present Help

God has set a high standard of holiness for us. He expects us to reach for that standard daily. The world, both Christian and non-Christian, expects high standards of Christians, though those expectations are much lower than God's.

However, despite those lower expectations from our fellow man, we Christians often fall short of even these expectations. In some ways, we live under a microscope, where we are subject to considerable criticism when we fall short.

To my mind, we should be held to a higher standard. Christ came to earth to set that standard with the conduct of His own life and His teachings through His three-year ministry. We learned from Him the characteristics of His mind and what He expects from us. His Sermon on the Mount is an incredible delivery of the expectations He has for His followers. Upon consulting the New Living Translation of the Holy Bible, we find this standard described in Matthew 5:1–11. The mind and character of Christ included the traits of peaceful, pure, gentle, steadfast, honest, merciful, humble, approachable, responsive, and alive to God continually. These qualities are what God expects of us, and we must strive each day to grow spiritually so that we might more effectively develop our capacity to reach for this standard.

But, as I mentioned earlier, God and Christ know that we human beings are imperfect and that we live in an imperfect world filled with temptations and difficulties of many sorts. Jesus never said that life would be a total picnic, and in fact He told us that we should expect tribulations throughout life.

The Greatest Leap of Your Life

Those troubles are why He promised the presence and power of the Holy Spirit to be with us and within us throughout our lives. As troubles challenge us, hone us, and refine us, the Holy Spirit lifts us, strengthens us, and carries us through them. The Holy Spirit, to the believer, is very real and powerful and is equal with God and Christ. He is our helper who provides strength, guidance, and insight to the attuned believer. His direct impact on the believer is immense.

When I was in my teens, I went to see a movie called *A Man Called Peter*. It was based on a book written by Peter Marshall's wife. Peter Marshall was the pastor of the New York Avenue Presbyterian Church, often called the church of the presidents. It is about two blocks from the White House. Reverend Marshall also received the prestigious designation of Chaplain of the Senate. What I remember from the movie was that, when Peter Marshall was selected as pastor to his church, attendance was off, and the church had lost its vitality and appeal to a broad base of Christians. Marshall was apparently a tremendous preacher and man of God that resonated in a very broad way to the community. He soon had filled the church to the point where Sundays were full and the overflow stood outside to hear his sermons over loudspeakers that had been assembled to meet the needs of those who couldn't get inside the church.

Regarding tribulations, Peter Marshall said, "God will not permit any troubles to come upon us unless He has a specific plan by which great blessing can come out of the difficulty." I, too, believe his statement to be true because of God's love for us. For this reason He has given to all believers the Holy Spirit to guide us in our lives in both good and difficult times. The Bible says, "The God of all grace, who hath called us unto his eternal glory by Christ Jesus, after that ye have suffered a while, make you perfect, establish, strengthen, settle you" (Peter 5:10 KJV) and "All things work together for good to them that love God" (Romans 8:28 KJV).

An Example of Ever-Present Help

I recently faced one of these difficult times when I was fired as the hospital's CEO after nearly thirty years. I was shocked when the chairman came to me late in the afternoon of December 8, 2006, and said to me that I would be finishing my tenure in seven weeks at the annual meeting on January 30, 2007. As he was going through his "the board is

The Greatest Leap of Your Life

badly divided on this" presentation, I truly said to myself: *Can this be a dream?*

This termination was a difficult thing to swallow. The only other time I got fired was when I was a teenage paperboy and I got into a heated discussion with one of my customers. I was working for an older friend, and he was the one that had to do the firing, following the customer's complaint to the newspaper. No doubt, I deserved what I got.

The hospital matter was much more difficult to accept. It seemed to make sense to no one save a few board members. The hospital had so many years of success that included an enviable record of positive bottom lines, strong employee and medical staff relationships, a strong and successful affiliation with one of the best healthcare systems in the country — New York Presbyterian — strong patient satisfaction scores year in and year out, and comparatively low debt following decades of adding to our plant, modernizing it, and developing major clinical programs for our patients.

I won't bore you with great detail. Suffice it to say that eighteen months earlier I had challenged a very strong board member on his opinion about our fundraising capability with successful New Yorkers who had populated our service area with their second homes. I felt he had been unduly influenced

The Greatest Leap of Your Life

by one of these individuals, whose wife had just been added to our board. At that time, we were considering a thirty-million-dollar addition to the hospital, and we all felt that our campaign goal ought to be one half of that amount, which was reachable only through a successful campaign with our New York friends. This board member had been convinced that we could expect only small donations from that group. This difference of opinion led to the board member's resignation as general campaign chairman, though he remained on the hospital board. Over the following eighteen months, to my great surprise, he was able to poison the well enough to force the chairman of the board to ask me to leave. I was surprised to see this man cave to the pressure, but a few other board members had eventually been brought into the fold through some careful orchestration by the offended board member and the chairman.

To put this event in proper perspective, I was fortunate that a number of factors mitigated the trauma that can come from this sort of thing and made it easier for me. First, I received a very good severance. I had planned to retire three years hence, and the hospital essentially made me economically whole on this plan. Secondly, I was as comfortable as could be those last seven weeks at the hospital because I

The Greatest Leap of Your Life

knew the quality of the job I had done and was still doing at the time, as did the employees and the medical staff. I knew that this decision wasn't about performance; it was about one board member's vendetta and a chairman who had lost his bearings or courage or perhaps both. Our employees were shocked and upset, and many members of the medical staff came to my office prepared to take on the board to reverse this decision. While this support was comforting, I urged my supporters not to do so for two selfish reasons. First, the severance had not been finalized, and secondly, I told them that at that point I couldn't work for this board's leadership because this blindsided scheme to remove me had broken the bond of trust.

While I had a strong comfort level around the hospital family during those final weeks, I had no way to offset the embarrassment of having this disgrace published in the papers and the community knowing that I had been fired. The hospital's reputation for growth and success was widespread. I'm sure at least some people must have questioned whether I had done something criminal to justify the action. The public part of this event was the hardest part to endure for my family and me. When you spend thirty years of hard, effective work for your hospital and community and then have it torn down, not over performance, but over one man's anger and eighteen-month vendetta, the loss is disappointing and tough to accept. I chose not to comment in the press and simply walked away following the annual meeting.

I believe I handled the situation the best I could. I think I made those around me feel as comfortable as possible, and I certainly worked hard and effectively on the seven-week transition. I received great strength from my wife Judy and my grown children. They were incredible. As great and powerful as that support was, the greatest source of strength for me was my faith. God was with me every step of the way. Because of that constant sense of strong support, I did not get discouraged, and I did what I could to encourage my hospital family as I left, just as they had done for me for thirty years, right to the end.

In gaining closure to this important situation in my life, I can tell you that the real life experience of growth in the Holy Spirit reinforces our faith, enabling it to grow stronger for the tests that come, and when tested, this strong foundation in our lives enables us to handle the biggest challenges that come our way from a position of strength. While I never reached out to those involved in this episode, I very soon forgave them. My life is the beneficiary of that forgiveness, because I never had a sense of revenge or continuing anger in me over this injustice. Handling it any differently would only have damaged me.

God has a plan for every one of us, His children. Knowing just what His plan is can sometimes be difficult. Hopefully as we grow and mature in our faith and grow closer to God through praying and reading the Bible, we will understand His plan for us and feel His ever-present help. I, frankly, am very reluctant to assume that we all are going to hear a direct message from God on the details of His plan. I think that such an assumption puts us at risk of thinking we have heard directly from Him, when we may be mistaken. What is important is to focus on attempting to grow each day in our faith and surrender to Him. I trust that, as I live one day at a time, He will lead me into His plan without my knowing ahead of time or hearing specifically from Him what His plan is. Perhaps that scenario is not the case for me or you. Perhaps indeed we someday will clearly know what His plan is. In the meantime, I intend to grow each day in Him to the best of my ability and leave the rest to Him.

In Summary – The Powerful Simplicity for the Leap

In summary, as complex as some of these concepts seem, up to this point in the book I have tried to emphasize the simplicity of the message from our infinite God of love. In the next few pages, let me attempt to encapsulate it.

God has created us in His image and has given us a free will that gives us the dual capacity to love as well as to sin. We have done both, but sin was becoming the big winner. God looked down and knew that we needed help to reverse this trend. He came down as divine man in the form of Jesus Christ, His Son. Jesus taught us how to live through His teachings and His example. Jesus had to die on the cross as punishment for our sins because God had to exact justice for our sins in order to forgive us because of His hatred of sin. The only reconciliation possible was that His perfect, sinless Son, whom He loved dearly, must be that substitute. This sacrifice became the only way for us to be justified and to gain this forgiveness. Our redemption is why Christ lived on earth and why He died.

But if the story were to end there, it would not be the truly powerful message that has endured for over two thousand years. Two more things had to happen. First, Christ rose from the dead, promising for the believer life more abundantly (spiritually) here on earth and life everlasting following our earthly death.

Secondly, knowing how prone we remain to sin, Christ promised to give us help every day in living lives where sin can become the exception rather than the practice of our lives. He sent the Holy Spirit, who resides in each one of us, once we have been born again by receiving Jesus Christ as our Lord and Savior. The Holy Spirit is the third part of the Trinity, and He is God as well. He lives inside of us to give us guidance, strength, and a great peace and joy that bring great anticipation to each new day. But we must work to be filled with the Holy Spirit continually. We facilitate His active presence through daily praying to God and reading His Word. This constant exercise maintains the strength of our faith and trust in Him. It reminds and reinforces what we believe and know, enabling us not only to love Him as our Savior, but also to serve Him as our Lord by helping and caring for others.

Jesus Christ is a fact. His life and teachings are fact. Thousands witnessed His ministry and recorded it in writing. His death and resurrection are facts. Jesus did die, but He rose from the dead. Thousands witnessed His resurrection and wrote about it. His body was never found.

The historical record of Jesus is not a myth or fairy tale. It is a true event willed by an infinite God that has an enormous love for every one of His children. He wants us to worship Him and find peace and joy in our lives here on earth and life eternally with Him following our earthly death. As we grow in our daily exercise with Him, we will feel His presence, His insight, and His strength, as well as His love that convinces us of His truth. Truly, this truth is the "Good News."

While the Good News exists, most certainly everyone hasn't and won't accept it. Impediments will always hinder people, some of which we have noted earlier in this book. Some might ask, "If God is all powerful, then why hasn't the whole world converted to Christianity? Or in the United States, where our founding fathers had a deep reverence for God and His direct involvement in the survival and development of our country, why does God increasingly seem to be dismissed as unimportant to our country?" These questions are logical, but they're not the focus for this book. I will say that God never intended to control us like robots. What He loves most about His creation is that He gave us a free will

The Greatest Leap of Your Life

to determine how we wished to live our lives and respond to Him. He does not want to lose any of us, and so He sent Christ to us. His greatest joy is when we freely love Him in return for what He has given us. He could not cherish this love if it was controlled, as opposed to freely given. Thus, while God could control everything, He chose not to control everything, including His children's free will to make important choices in life.

He gave us intelligence to enjoy living and working and hopefully making wise decisions. Obviously, we have many failures on the books, as history shows. We have lost our way on many occasions, and in compromises made within our society, we have many times relegated God to a far distant second place. Sometimes pushing God aside has been easier than standing up to the forces in our politics and society that push God and His love to the sideline.

Despite this record, God still forgives and loves us and looks forward to us, as individuals, receiving His Good News and living it daily in our lives. When we do so, irrespective of the environment around us, we can make our world a better place, whether in our homes, communities, workplaces, or our country. We can make our surroundings better, no matter what compromise has preceded us. God wants us to be strong and happy in this world, and through faith in His love and strength, we can and will make a difference in this world that may impact one or many people and situations in our lives. May God continue to bless us all in our journey in what I consider the greatest leap of my life, and I hope in yours as well!

In the final chapter, I discuss the second coming of Jesus Christ. For those of you who have now made the great leap, this astounding future event will not be as difficult to understand or accept as it will likely be for others. For those people who still doubt God's plan of salvation for His children, this discussion is likely to appear as just another foolish tale. Here again is where accepting the distinction between infinite and finite becomes important. Only an infinite God with infinite wisdom could plan the birth of Christ, His resurrection after death, and His second coming.

Chapter IX

The Second Coming of Christ

How many times have you heard the following phrases: "They talk about him as if he's the second coming," or "The way they describe her abilities, you'd think she walks on water." I don't particularly appreciate hearing such descriptions applied to individuals because they take license with a reference to Jesus Christ and lend a bit of mockery to Him. Whether my opinion is a bit narrow minded or just a reflection of the love I have for what He has done for me throughout my life, I don't want Him disparaged in any way.

The greater point to be made is that the context brought out in such statements reflects in the speaker an assessment of another human being, attributing to him characteristics of supernatural proportions. Somehow, even to the non-believer, the traits and characteristics of Christ as expressed in the Bible appear miraculous, unusual, or incredibly significant. This view is yet another reflection on the value of understanding the clear distinction in the capacity of an infinite God and finite mankind.

God's plan for our salvation through Jesus Christ and the Holy Spirit is powerful and almost unimaginable. Our finite minds cannot fully comprehend the depth of God's love for us.

The Growth of Christianity and the Holy Spirit

Just think of the extraordinary power that had to be associated with the rise of Christianity from some two thousand years ago to today. When Jesus came to earth in accord with clear predictions in several sections of the Old Testament, some who believed that the Messiah was coming could not accept Jesus as the Messiah. They expected the Messiah to be a king-warrior, along the lines of David, and to conquer the world for His followers. They were looking for a return of an earthly kingdom similar to that of Solomon. Fulfilling that expectation was not Jesus' mission two thousand years ago.

Jesus made this point very clear in His exchange with Pilate. Pilate asked, "Are you the King of the Jews?" (John 18:33 TLB). Jesus answered, "I am not an earthly King. If I were, my followers would have fought when I was arrested by the Jewish leaders. But my Kingdom is not of this world." Pilate responded: "But you are a King there?" Jesus then replied: "Yes, I was born for that purpose. And I come to bring the truth to the world. All who love the truth are my followers" (John 18: 36-38 TLB).

The disciples themselves temporarily adopted the expectation of the Jews of that day that Jesus was about to become an earthly King. T.W. Hunt described this hope in *The Mind of Christ* in a scene following Christ's death:

> The disciples observed the Sabbath; the priests did not. The priests went to Pilate and informed him of Jesus' claim that He would rise again after three days. These enemies of Jesus remembered something that the disciples had forgotten. Somehow, although He had predicted these events all along, His disciples had not been able to take in their reality and meaning. They had been blinded by their hopes for an immediate earthly kingdom. Because of their encounters with Jesus' incredible power, their attention had been fixed on a worldly glory, so much so that Jesus' words did not sink in. Their enemies were more cunning (wickedness always is). The priests

and the Pharisees wanted to safeguard what they believed to be their accomplishment.

The priests asked Pilate for a guard to keep the disciples from stealing the body and then claiming that Jesus had been resurrected from the dead. Pilate told them that they had a guard and ordered the securing of the tomb. They placed a seal, probably clay or wax, on the two stones so that any disturbance would be immediately apparent—and Jesus Christ became the first person in history to be guarded to keep Him in His grave.

This Sabbath was the most difficult day in the life of the eleven disciples and the small group of women. First of all, they were grieving profoundly. Never had they known a love like Jesus had shown them (John 13:1, 15:9).

Second, they were extremely disappointed. From the beginning, in spite of Jesus' repeated emphasis on the spiritual nature of His kingdom, they had envisaged what every Jew of the time had imagined—a conquering Messiah to expel Rome from Palestine and set up a splendid, visible political kingdom like that of Solomon. Even as late as the night of the betrayal, they were quarreling over their relative greatness in that new government. These high hopes were now dashed. The hated Romans had succeeded in putting to death the man they thought was invincible.

Eleven disciples were left after the crucifixion of Christ, and their sorrow and disappointment were deep and bitter. But through Christ's resurrection and the days leading up to the Holy Spirit appearing, the disciples remembered three major things. Christ had died as a representation and substitute for the past, present, and future sins of mankind. He had risen to prove victory over death. And He would return again someday to reign. They began a great movement (Christianity) that has had more positive impact on the quality of people's lives than any other movement in history.

Paul records a poignant moment in Christian history and its growth in the book of Acts in the New Testament. Peter and the apostles had been warned and arrested a number of times for preaching about Jesus. They were arrested again and told once again to stop. Peter addressed his accusers in the following excerpt from Acts 5:29–39 NLT.

> But Peter and the apostles replied, "We must obey God rather than human authority. The God of our ancestors raised Jesus from the dead after you killed him by crucifying him. Then God put him in the place of honor at his right hand as Prince and Savior. He did this to give the people of Israel an opportunity to turn from their sins and turn to God so their sins would be forgiven. We are witnesses of these things and so is the Holy Spirit, who is given by God to those who obey him."
> At this, the high council was furious and decided to kill them. But one member had a different perspective. He was a Pharisee named Gamaliel, who was an expert on religious law and was very popular

with the people. He stood up and ordered that the apostles be sent outside the council chamber for a while. Then he addressed his colleagues as follows: "Men of Israel, take care what you are planning to do to these men! Some time ago there was that fellow Theudas, who pretended to be someone great. About four hundred others joined him, but he was killed, and his followers went their various ways. The whole movement came to nothing. After him, at the time of the census, there was Judas of Galilee. He got some people to follow him, but he was killed, too, and all his followers were scattered.

"So my advice is, leave these men alone. If they are teaching and doing these things merely on their own, it will soon be overthrown. But if it is of God, you will not be able to stop them. You may even find yourselves fighting against God."

The council accepted his advice.

Gamaliel's advice turned out to be a wise prophesy that seemed improbable at the time. The Christian message must have seemed surreal. The opposition was staggering. Against such odds then and through the centuries, this small band of men and women could not have started Christianity and then taken it, with new converts and leaders over time, to its enormous growth of today without the power and guidance of God and the Holy Spirit.

Christ's impact on the world goes beyond our salvation and the peace of mind that His sacrifice has brought millions of believers. His teachings are also a significant basis for what Christians and non-Christians have done through the last two millennia to improve the lot of mankind socially, politically, ethically, and spiritually. Their actions are a major part of what is often noted as the influence of the Judeo-Christian ethic, reflected through the Old and New Testaments of the Bible.

The Final Piece – Christ's Second Coming

The final piece of God's plan is yet to come, and we do not know when it will occur. But Christ told us He would return. His return is mentioned over one hundred times in the New Testament. Here are excerpts from Jesus' description of this event from Matthew 24:3-43 in The Living Bible.

> And as he sat upon the Mount of Olives, the disciples came unto him privately, saying, Tell us, when shall these things be? and what shall be the sign of thy coming, and of the end of the world?
> And Jesus answered and said unto them, Take heed that no man deceive you.
> For many shall come in my name, saying, I am Christ; and shall deceive many.
> And ye shall hear of wars and rumours of wars; see that ye be not troubled: for all these things must come to pass, but the end is not yet.

For nation shall rise against nation, and kingdom against kingdom: and there shall be famines, and pestilences, and earthquakes, in divers places.

All these are the beginning of sorrows.

Then shall they deliver you up to be afflicted, and shall kill you: and ye shall be hated of all nations for my name's sake.

And then shall many be offended, and shall betray one another, and shall hate one another.

And many false prophets shall rise, and shall deceive many.

And because iniquity shall abound, the love of many shall wax cold.

But he that shall endure unto the end, the same shall be saved.

And this gospel of the kingdom shall be preached in all the world for a witness unto all nations; and then shall the end come. ...

For then shall be great tribulation, such as was not since the beginning of the world to this time, no, nor ever shall be.

And except those days should be shortened, there should no flesh be saved: but for the elect's sake those days shall be shortened.

Then if any man shall say unto you, Lo, here is Christ, or there; believe it not.

For there shall arise false Christs, and fake prophets, and shall shew great signs and wonders; insomuch that, if it were possible, they shall deceive the very elect.

Behold, I have told you before.

Wherefore if they shall say unto you, Behold, he is in the desert; go not forth: behold, he is in the secret chambers; believe it not.

The Greatest Leap of Your Life

For as the lightning cometh out of the east, and shineth even unto the west, so shall also the coming of the Son of man be.

Immediately after the tribulation of those days shall the sun be darkened, and the moon shall not give her light, and the stars shall fall from heaven, and the powers of the heavens shall be shaken:

And then shall appear the sign of the Son of man in heaven: and then shall all the tribes of the earth mourn, and they shall see the Son of man coming in the clouds of heaven with power and great glory.

And he shall send his angels with a great sound of a trumpet, and they shall gather together his elect from the four winds, from one end of heaven to the other.

Now learn a parable of the fig tree; When his branch is yet tender, and putteth forth leaves, ye know that summer is nigh:

So likewise ye, when ye shall see all these things, know that it is near, even at the doors.

Verily I say unto you, This generation shall not pass, till all these things be fulfilled.

Heaven and earth shall pass away, but my words shall not pass away.

But of that day and hour knoweth no man, no, not the angels of heaven, but my Father only.

But as the days of Noe were, so shall also the coming of the Son of man be.

For as in the days that were before the flood they were eating and drinking, marrying and giving in marriage, until the day that Noe entered into the ark,

And knew not until the flood came, and took them all away; so shall also the coming of the Son of man be. ...

> Watch therefore: for ye know not what hour your Lord doth come.
>
> But know this, that if the goodman of the house had known in what watch the thief would come, he would have watched, and would not have suffered his house to be broken up.
>
> Therefore be ye also ready: for in such an hour as ye think not the Son of man cometh.

While Christ warned against speculating on the time when He would return, His second coming is predicted throughout Scripture. He said the following in Luke 21:28 KJV: "When these things begin to come to pass, then look up, and lift up your heads; for your redemption draweth nigh."

To some, perhaps many, the second coming of Jesus Christ is just another of those implausible aspects of Christianity that discourage people from taking that leap of faith. Some say that Christianity is a form of escapism, as we noted earlier in this book. Some feel that Christians deal with the surreal and aren't willing to deal with the life in a real way.

C. S. Lewis noted, to the contrary, the following in his book *Mere Christianity*:

> "Hope is one of the theological virtues. This means that a continual looking forward to the eternal world is not, as some modern people think, a form of

escapism or wishful thinking, but one of the things a Christian is meant to do. It does not mean that we are to leave the present world as it is. If you read history, you will find that the Christians who did most for the present world were just those who thought most of the next. It is since Christians have largely ceased to think of the other world that they have become so ineffective in this. Aim at heaven and you will get earth thrown in. Aim at earth and you will get neither."

Response to Cynics about the Second Coming

The question cynics often raise is: "Why has the second coming been so long in coming?" John MacArthur discusses that question on page 57 of his book *The Second Coming*:

> How can it be, then, that 2,000 years later Christ still has not returned? Could the apostles have been in error about the timing? That is precisely what some skeptics claim. Here's a typical excerpt from a newsletter whose sole aim is to attack the inerrancy of Scripture:
>
>> Paul, himself, showed ... that he was among those who awaited the imminent return of Christ. Yet, as the history of that era clearly shows, all was for nought. No messiah appeared. ... The NT repeatedly says the messiah was to return in a very short time. Yet, mankind has waited for nearly 2,000 years and nothing has occurred. By no stretch

of the imagination can that be considered "coming quickly." ... It is, indeed, unfortunate that millions of people still cling to the forlorn hope that somehow a messiah will arise to extract them from their predicament. How many years (2,000, 10,000, 100,000) will it take for them to finally say, "We can only conclude that we are the victims of a cruel hoax"?

I have no doubt that Christ will return. He stated that He would, and I accept His word as truth. He clearly indicated that He wouldn't reappear until the "gospel of the Kingdom shall be preached in all the world for a witness unto all nations." We are very close to that reality. However, my affirmation of my belief does not convince others. I would like, however, to make a couple of points here. Christ gave a lengthy description of the many things that must happen before His return, yet He warned about speculating on the exact time. Instead, He said that we should be watchful and ready. The second part which skeptics miss is that what's more important than the date of His second coming is what we do with our short lives prior to death. For God and Christ will hold everyone accountable either at death, for those who die before He comes, or at the time of Christ's return, for those still alive then. I consider it far more important to decide on Christ as our Lord and Savior within our relatively short lifetimes rather than focus on whether His return is ten years or ten thousand years from now.

For me the fact that Jesus will return again doesn't seem as significant, because I believe I am already saved through my faith that Jesus died for my sins and came back to life to assure us of life eternal in paradise with Him. But God's plan calls for Jesus to return, and therefore His return is a very important part of Christianity. Perhaps this element to God's plan will somehow awaken to the truth of salvation through Christ some of His children that might not have been touched otherwise. God loves us so much that He wants all of us through our free will to worship Him and to accept Jesus as our Lord and Savior. He doesn't want to lose any of us to hell and damnation.

We are a stubborn and selfish group of human beings when left to our own devices. We sometimes only get religion when we are threatened in some fashion that touches us or our loved ones. God has promised that each man is to die once, and afterwards we no longer have an opportunity to accept Christ's salvation. The Bible warned the people of Noah's days: "My Spirit shall not always strive with man" (Genesis 6:3 KJV). Beginning with John the Baptist, many pastors, priests, and others have argued that now is the time to repent before it is too late. They emphasize that judgment is near, as Christ will be returning soon. As noted above, some look upon this argument with skepticism, because two thousand years has passed since Christ's death and He hasn't returned. Christ could come tomorrow, several months from now, in ten years, or two centuries from now. We just don't know. What the skeptics think, as noted in the above newsletter, overlooks that our last chance to repent for our sinful ways and accept Jesus as our Lord and Savior could come much sooner than Christ's second coming. When we die or become mentally incapacitated, we have lost our opportunity for salvation with God and Christ if we haven't accepted Him as our Lord and Savior before then, irrespective of when Jesus returns to earth. This point, to me, is so incredibly important that I'm tempted to repeat it several times on this page!

Perhaps God's plan for Jesus returning is that some of the people who are harder to convince will be affected sometime in their life by this truth or fear, that have not previously been touched by Christ. I simply do not know what our infinite Creator had in mind with this great promise. But I fully trust that every element of His plan exists to give each of

The Greatest Leap of Your Life

us the best possible chance to find and accept our Lord and Savior before we lose the opportunity. The New Testament refers to the second coming of Jesus Christ over one hundred times. This return is His promise.

Then, of course, there is the skepticism of Christ revealing that He will be visible to all when He returns and that there will be absolutely no doubt in our minds that it is Him returning. These skeptics say, "How can He be seen everywhere at the same time?" Yes, here is another example for the critics to call Christianity surreal.

Well, I don't have the specific answer. But my faith allows me to believe what He said. Furthermore, this objection gets back to the power of an infinite God to achieve whatever He chooses. If half the world can see the same sun at the same time on any given day, I can believe that our Father in heaven is capable of having his Son return to earth, visible to all, leaving no doubt about His return and the fulfillment of His promise.

Will We Be Ready?

One thing I can promise you is that, as you grow and mature as a Christian, you truly come closer to God, Christ, and the Holy Spirit. In that growth, you become stronger in your faith because you feel the presence, strength, and insight given to you through the Holy Spirit. This growth becomes a foundation built on rock rather than sand, guides you through difficult times, and enlightens you to know that Jesus spoke the truth in everything He said. It also broadens your horizons of care and concern for others in your life and helps you to love your neighbor, your family, and even your enemies.

Trusting this provision and loving Him for His sacrifice for us helps us grow each day in the depth of our faith and love for Him and gives us the strength and guidance to take on the challenges of life and overcome our fears. I recall one time being very anxious about something difficult I was facing, and that morning I read Mark 4:40 NLT where Jesus turned to the disciples after quieting the wind and sea and asked them, "Why are you so afraid? Do you still not have faith in me?" I was touched by the truth of Christ's presence always through the Holy Spirit and immediately felt at peace with renewed faith to address what was before me. I promise you that He has a way of always being present for His children, if we will only trust Him.

When we are prepared through our trust and faith to meet Him at our death or His second coming, we will not be afraid. In his letters, John sums it up nicely (1 John 4:13–17 NLT):

> And God has given us his Spirit as proof that we live in him and he in us.
> Furthermore, we have seen with our own eyes and now testify that the Father sent his Son to be the Savior of the world. All who proclaim that Jesus is the Son of God have God living in them, and they live in God. We know how much God loves us, and we have put our trust in him.
> God is love, and all who live in love live in God, and God lives in them. And as we live in God, our love grows more perfect. So we will not be afraid on the day of judgment, but we can face him with confidence because we are like Christ here in this world.

Such love has no fear because "perfect love expels all fear."

May God bless us all with His wisdom and love and lead us all to find eternal life through our faith in Jesus Christ, before it is too late. May He guide us all in taking the greatest leap of our lives.

Epilogue

What I have attempted to do with this book is to provide, as a layman, a simple and relatively short summary of a complex subject. In so doing, I have lengthened it a bit with some repetitions that I believe can reinforce for the reader key components of God's plan for salvation.

As a helpful, practical aid, I recommend four or five routines that an individual can practice to find and live this faith as described in the book. I do so in the Epilogue as an appropriate conclusion to the preceding Preface, Introduction, and nine chapters.

First you have to come to grips with whether you believe in an infinite Supreme Being, God. I have spent some time in this book discussing the contrary obstacles in life that can make it difficult for mankind to accept that something exists that is greater than we human beings. My church's pastor, Dr. Craig McClellan, recently attended a forum in Hartford, Connecticut, entitled: "The God Is/Is Not Great Debate." The speakers and panelists were three well-known people: an atheist, a rabbi, and a divinity professor. This experience caused him to deliver a sermon on this topic shortly thereafter. In his sermon, he summarized positions by Freud and the atheist speaker that help to define some of the challenges that we face in taking that leap into belief in an infinite God.

Freud's position is that we transfer anxieties and a sense of terror about this world from childhood; hence we rely on our earthly father (parents) to protect us from our anguish. Then as adults, we experience more of the same anxiety and look for a heavenly Father to do the same. Thus religion is a coping mechanism to deal with life and death. The position of the atheist at this forum was that religion and the church define human beings as bad children, unworthy and inferior, and that religion attempts to control our minds and fears, causing us to feel a need for a God in our lives in order to restore some self-esteem. This particular atheist not only dismisses Christ as the Son of God but also believes that Christ never existed, but was invented by the church. This philosophy is just a sample of the criticism and obstacles that exist as barriers against our accepting as fact the existence of God and taking that great leap of faith necessary to begin and develop that relationship.

If you do accept the existence of God, what do you know of His expectations of us? First, if you believe in the Bible as I do, then you attempt to learn something of God's expectations there. I believe that the Old and New Testaments were written by men guided by God and therefore contain many of God's expectations. I admit that I personally focus primarily on the New Testament.

Secondly, the New Testament tells us of God's plan for salvation through His Son, Jesus Christ. The four Gospels of Matthew, Mark, Luke, and John tell us much about Jesus' ministry, teachings, and example. I would recommend that you focus initially on these four Gospels and even reread them a number of times. Start with a chapter or a few subheadings a day, and reflect on what you've read. These relatively short but powerful Gospels include much truth. Mark was the first written and John the last. They cover in detail the following important aspects of Christ's life: His teachings, example, sacrificial death, and resurrection. Again, I advocate reading short segments at a time and reflecting on their meaning rather than reading a lot at one time with no reflection upon what's been read.

Thirdly, simultaneously or shortly after these two steps, you will begin praying daily. Hopefully, as you progress, you will grow in your understanding of God's true plan of salvation for all of us, and you will accept Jesus as your Lord and Savior. When you do, the Holy Spirit will come into your heart to guide and strengthen you. This true acceptance provides an inherent, awesome love that provides great loyalty, faith, and strength to the believer and causes him to become over time a new person filled with great peace and joy.

Fourthly, and very importantly, you must consistently exercise your mind and heart each day through praying and reading the Bible to enhance your growth and maturity. Know that you will stumble along the way, as all humans are still imperfect. But don't ever be discouraged about any lapse for long. Just as a baby must crawl before walking and walk before running, so too, the newly born-again Christian must reinforce on a daily basis what he has accepted as the truth in order to advance his growth from a beginning Christian to a walking and running Christian. Your resilient faith and trust brings with it the continual flow of the Holy Spirit filling your heart with a sense of perspective and insight and a growing and sustaining faith. This power continues to grow and allows your new way of life to become more natural, vibrant, and real as each day passes.

You will gradually orient your mind and desires to the mind of Christ, which includes greater patience, compassion, peace, joy, and love for those around you. With this growth, you will go from practicing sin in your life to eliminating sin until it is more the exception than the rule and your mind and thoughts are much more charitable and caring than ever before. The timing of this transition will vary among born-again Christians. But as it comes, you will find a new excitement, anticipation, and peace in your life that you have never felt before.

Finally, continue to exercise spiritually these habits that will maintain the strength, endurance, and consistency of your faith. Thus, once you have made this decision to leap forward, maintaining and developing this change by the exercising of your mind heart and soul with that of the Holy Spirit is now just as important. The Spirit will always help you and bring greater clarity for you in this new and exciting greatest leap of your life.

This work of the Holy Spirit is so important in our lives going forward because an infinite God's plan for salvation

The Greatest Leap of Your Life

through Jesus Christ appears so surreal to many that it's sometimes difficult to see the forest for the trees. We have all seen beautiful embroidery during our lives with its clear needlework patterns. Have you ever looked at the back of that embroidery? What you see is not a clear pattern, but only the patchwork evidence of what's on the other side. God sees the clear side of life that is best for those whom He has created. On our own, we see the disjointed, patchwork side of life. God, through the Holy Spirit, brings new awareness to the believer of what God sees for us in the embroidery of life that is best for all of us.

Finally, let us remember that, while we are to avoid getting entangled in the world and all its distractions, we are clearly obligated to be part of the world and to do our best to live what we believe, while making the world a better place to live through our relationships, time, talents, and charity. We are responsible, despite our imperfections, to reflect genuinely to others the impact that God, Christ, and the Holy Spirit have had on our lives so that we, with God's guidance, may lead others to make the greatest leap of their lives.

Sources

Funk and Wagnalls Standard Dictionary, Vols. 1&2. New York: Harper & Row, 1984.

Funk and Wagnalls New Encyclopedia. Vol. 14. New York: Funk and Wagnalls L.P. Publishers, 1986.

Graham, Billy. *Unto the Hills*. Dallas: Word Publishing, 1996.

Hunt, T. W. *The Mind of Christ*. Nashville: Broadman and Holman, 1995.

Lewis, C. S. *Mere Christianity*. New York: Macmillan Publishers, 1952.

MacArthur, John F. *The Second Coming*. Wheaton: Crossway Books Publishing, 1999.

Maraniss, David. *When Pride Still Mattered*. New York: Touchstone Paperback, Simon and Schuster Publishers, 1999.